T0357738

'James and Liz have put their finge
– particularly in the rising generati
leadership: we are aware of the fai.
leadership, often played out in public, and only too aware of our
own shortcomings. But the world needs leaders! *Normal, Imperfect
Heroes* reminds us that through his transformational grace, God
raises up and uses unlikely people for his purposes. I pray that this
book will encourage a surge of leaders to step forward humbly but
confidently.'
Archie Coates, Vicar, HTB

'In the midst of a noisy world, every so often a fresh voice appears
that is worth stopping our restless activity to listen to. One that
speaks old things in new ways. In this case it is a dual voice – an
amalgam of husband and wife. An activist and a thinker. A joker
and a priest. It works spectacularly well. They find a sweet spot that
narrates their shared story of ministry but also their shared gleaning
from the flawed, yet inspiring stories of the leaders of Scripture.
In the midst of their glorious and at times comedic honesty, you
might just find a way through our present crises of trust, leadership
and polarisation. The Griers allow us a window into a world where
imperfection, disagreement and embrace can co-exist by boldly
letting us into theirs.'
Andy Flannagan, Executive Director, Christians in Politics

'James and Liz brilliantly unpack biblical characters and their stories
with humour and sensitivity throughout. I found the wise insights
and reflections weaved into the stories challenging and helpful and
am sure this book will be both a great encouragement to many from
those starting out in faith to those who have been walking with Jesus
a long time. A great resource tackling important issues for a time just
like this.'
Paul Friend, Director, South West Youth Ministries (SWYM)

'Grounded, real and at times humorous. James and Liz have written a thought-provoking and challenging exploration of some of the best-known characters in the Bible. Flawed and fallible, we discover we are all of infinite value to a God who loves us regardless.'
Justin Humphreys, joint CEO, Thirtyone:eight

'James and Liz present a gloriously humbling and encouraging view of what it is to lead in Jesus' Kingdom. Benefitting from their rich study of Scripture and years of experience, the book is full of examples of flawed people achieving momentous things through God. It is a reminder that, even when we feel like failures, God is bigger. And that is a reminder we all need regularly.'
Rt Revd Dr Emma Ineson, Bishop of Kensington

'I have been privileged to have seen the remarkable ministry of Bishop James and Liz Grier. James (with Liz's help) has given an intriguing look at some of the flawed heroes of the Bible with delightful touches of humour to carry the lessons to be learned.'
Canon David MacInnes, Former Rector, St Aldate's Church, Oxford

'To slightly paraphrase Mark Twain; "The best cure for Christian leadership is reading the Bible". [He actually said, "The best cure for Christianity is reading the Bible."]

'We have lived through watershed years, where church leadership has been weighed and found wanting. Where we might turn for a reset? The services of many coaches, management gurus and motivational experts have been employed. What James and Liz do, for a hundredth of the price, is that thing which is strangely lacking – they address the soul of godly leadership by opening the Bible and giving it freedom to address our lives.

'In dynamic and incisive studies of these high complex and flawed leaders, they bring out direct applications to our lives, our patterns and our practices of leading and that to which we hope and aspire. The leadership experts might do us some good, but if we spend time

in the Griers' company as they open God's word, we will not only save money, the Lord might just save our souls.'
Canon Chris Russell, Archbishop's Advisor for Evangelism and Witness

'Imposter syndrome can crush us, but the good news is that it's usually built on a misunderstanding of leadership. The most encouraging realisation for any leader is that they walk in the footsteps not of perfect, flawless giants of faith, skill and character, but of profoundly *normal* people – and that's the compelling central point of this wonderful book. We've all heard the assertion that God chooses regular people like you and me to change the world, and allowed it to wash over us; this book dives deep into stories that confront us with the reality. In his divine and extraordinary grace, God sees our flaws and uses us anyway.'
Martin Saunders, author of *We Are Satellites* and *Signal Fire*

'James and Liz's book comes at a cultural moment when we need honest and more nuanced conversations about the nature of human brokenness in the context of Christian leadership. This hope-filled book is full of the Grier's own hard-worn pastoral experience alongside biblical insights from less-than-ideal-leaders. They give comfort and challenge in equal measure.'
Revd Pete Norris, Location Pastor, Gas Street, Birmingham

'*Normal, Imperfect Heroes* is the leadership book we all need; biblical, practical, simple and relatable. James and Liz have opened up Scripture, and their lives, to show us how God can work through the challenge of our pasts, our character flaws and even our greatest mistakes. It is both an inspiring and humbling read that reaffirms the foundations of good and godly leadership.

'It is a must read for anyone involved in Christian leadership. Biblical and practical, it reaffirms the redeeming and powerful work of God, in and through our broken lives.'
Revd Will Van Der Hart, Director, Mind and Soul Foundation

'Reading this book is like taking an inspiring and refreshing walk with Liz and James. Their humanity, honesty and deep spirituality shines through ringing warmth, encouragement and reality. The lessons BM made visible from these familiar lives are life changing and life affirming.'
David Westlake, Chief Executive Officer, IJM UK

'In this honest reflection James and Liz tap into something of the zeitgeist of the age to offer us scripturally based wisdom with ready and sensible application for aspiring and practicing leaders. The perspectives offered show scripture not as a 'quick fix' to questions of leadership, but the source of inspiration and example to delve deeply into. This book will be helpful wherever you are on your own journey of leadership, as you journey with normal, imperfect heroes.'
Revd Russell Winfield, Dean of St Mellitus College

'*Normal, Imperfect Heroes* contains both challenge and encouragement to follow Jesus faithfully in whatever position of influence and leadership we might have. And ultimately, James and Liz remind us that failure and weakness don't have the final word – God very much does.'
Emma Worrall, Open Doors UK

'In the normal, imperfect, messy journey of my own life and ministry, James and Liz Grier have been kind and most generous companions. They've walked with me through many chapters of my story, and in this book, they walk with us through the stories of many of the "heroes" of Scripture, unpacking the truth and wisdom of Bible characters with fresh authority. Ultimately, this book gives a fresh revelation of the free and generous love of Jesus, the only unfailing hero.'
Canon Sarah Yardley, writer, speaker, evangelist, Lectio 365 contributor

James is a Devon boy and hugely proud of it. He still can't quite believe that God has brought him home to be Bishop of Plymouth. He's married to Liz, the beauty and brains of the marriage, and they have two fantastic sons, Josh and Toby, and a wonderful daughter-in-law, Rebeccah. He's been ordained for over half his life and in that time they have served in large urban churches, small rural ones and started a church to reach young people with little or no experience of faith.

Liz is married to James and has the same children. She's also author of another book, *Beginning Unlimited* (Instant Apostle, 2018). She's a scientist, harpist and theologian. When she's not being clever, she'll be sea swimming!

NORMAL, IMPERFECT HEROES

The stories of biblical leaders who are
more like you and me than we realise

James Grier
With Liz Grier

FORM

First published in Great Britain in 2025

SPCK
SPCK Group
Studio 101
The Record Hall
16–16A Baldwin's Gardens
London EC1N 7RJ
www.spckpublishing.co.uk

British Library Cataloguing-in-Publication Data
A catalogue record for this book is available from the British Library

ISBN 978–0–281–09098–3
eBook ISBN 978–0–281–09099–0

1 3 5 7 9 10 8 6 4 2

Typeset by Fakenham Prepress Solutions, Fakenham, Norfolk NR21 8NL

eBook by Fakenham Prepress Solutions, Fakenham, Norfolk NR21 8NL

Produced on paper from sustainable sources

Dedication

To the next generation, and three of them in particular: Josh, Toby and Rebeccah. You don't need to be perfect. We love you just as you are, but pray that you will be free to be all that God has made you to be.

Contents

Prologue   xii

Foreword by Liz   xiv

Introduction   xvii

Part 1
THE BEGINNINGS OF LEADERSHIP

1   The father of faith   3

2   The hustler   20

3   Favourite child   36

Part 2
THE PRINCE OF EGYPT

4   The prince of Egypt   55

Part 3
THE TALE OF TWO KINGS

5   Saul   91

6   David   115

Part 4
TWELVE GOOD MEN

7   The disciples   151

8   The women in Jesus' life   187

Conclusion: What about us?   194

Acknowledgements   197

Prologue

Several years ago, I began writing this book on sabbatical but never quite managed to finish it. At the stage when it still needed a lot more work, I put it to one side and it simply became an oft-quoted anecdote: the one where I'd written a book around failure that I'd failed to get published. It seems timely that I am returning to this project in 2024 as both within Christian circles and wider culture, many high-profile leaders have been exposed as not being all we had believed. This has raised questions for those of us who admired them and benefited from their leadership. Many have felt betrayed and misled, disappointed and angry, but also – if you're anything like me – confused about God. Why did he let them lead in the first place? Why did he apparently bless their leadership, only for people to be hurt by them? Is there any worth in any of their ministry, or is it all tainted and therefore to be dismissed? Such emotions aren't helped by today's cancel culture, where any kind of failure means that people, and everything about them, are written off.

As I wrestled with these questions, and more, I found myself returning again and again to the leaders we read about in Scripture. You see, God has always chosen broken, messed-up people to be his leaders. In fact, I am drawn to the biblical leaders precisely because of all their faults and failings. I've found myself captivated by the adopted prince, Moses; by the first kings, Saul and David, and then the elite team Jesus chose to be his band of disciples and leaders. This book is the product of my reflections on them.

I returned to this abandoned manuscript at the urging of my wife, Liz. She convinced me that my reflections were worth sharing and, perhaps more importantly, offered to join me in the venture. When Liz was eight months pregnant with our first child we moved to Birmingham. One memorable weekend, her DIY-savvy dad and I built most of a bookcase in our new home. When he had to go home, I was left to finish the assembly on my own. In desperation, I roped in my heavily pregnant wife. She was amazing and with her help I actually finished it. On completion I famously said that she had been 'reasonably useful' – something I have never lived down. Since I first began this book, Liz has gained a masters in theology, been ordained and has started a PhD … and that's just in her spare time. We also led a church plant together in Exeter for over ten years and she wrote and published a book about it, *Beginning Unlimited* (Instant Apostle, 2018). So her input to my original manuscript has been more than 'reasonably useful'. In fact, it's totally transformed it. The original thoughts and reflections are mine, but Liz has rewritten bits into coherent English; improved (and, begrudgingly I'll admit, corrected) my theology; added better analogies and even turned some of my attempts at humour into genuinely funny interjections. This book has remained in my voice, to avoid confusion and for readability, but at times the point being made will be hers. Those points are easy to spot – they're the good ones!

I pray that as you join me in reflecting on these unlikely heroes you will find yourself captivated and challenged, like I have been, by all that they can teach us through their lives, their inspirational successes and their ignominious failings. Throughout it all, God's steadfast and faithful love remains constant.

Interspersed with the biblical stories are some reflections from our ministry, where we have prayed with so many incredible people. Our commitment to prayer, and indeed our whole life vision, is a longing to see people set free from everything that hinders and the sin that so easily entangles, helping them fix their eyes on Jesus, who has made a way for us to be in relationship with God our Father, who loves his children deeply.

James Grier

A foreword by Liz

Every section of this book is male dominated. This happened in part by accident. Our reflections originate from reflecting, teaching and preaching on the people the Bible focuses in on the most. Lauren, our editor, challenged us to include the women, but we found we had a problem. Not because the women aren't there. They are everywhere in Scripture, even if centuries of church history have focused on the males. Women in Scripture, however, are not such a mixture of strength and weakness as the men. They tend to be either total villains like Jezebel or complete heroes like the Virgin Mary. We only catch slight glimpses of the flaws of the women in Scripture compared to the men. What we began to recognise was that in the women's stories there is a completely different focus.

As we will see, the Bible thoroughly deconstructs its male characters. It is not an instruction manual that we can just take, read and apply to our own lives. We need to wrestle with and think about what it is telling us. Take, for example, Moses, who is remembered as an incredible leader and prophet who spoke face to face with God. But when we read his backstory, he was all too human in his fears and failings. Perhaps the biggest lesson we learn from his life is that he succeeded, not because of who he was, but because of who was with him. But where Moses is revealed in all his insecurity and failing, the five women of Exodus 2 are totally positively characterised.

The women throughout Scripture lived in a context that was patriarchal. Women were often treated as property. They were owned, used and sadly sometimes abused by their families. The stories of the women are vital and they need to be listened to. They highlight how we should challenge leadership from a place of powerlessness. This is not true for every woman in Scripture, as some did lead and exercise incredible ministries. But if we just take, for example, the five women in the genealogy of Jesus, they are significant precisely because of how they lived from their lowly positions. Jewish culture would have expected them to be written out of God's story because of their identity, yet God wrote them into the very heart of it.

The stories of the men, as this book has highlighted, show their weakness. Predominantly the women in Scripture show their leadership and strength. Both positions are counter-cultural. Women didn't need to be seen as any lower. Scripture challenges society's perception of women while, ironically, widely being held responsible for this viewpoint. Today there is still much to challenge about the way society perceives and treats women.

We also mustn't reduce women to a two dimensional representation. The women were complex too, and don't present female followers of Jesus today with easy role models. Rachel lied about being on her period, Rebecca and Rachel caused problems with their favouritism, Sarah was deeply cynical and bitter, Naomi was co-dependant and probably played into her victim mentality. And there is so much are not told. Was Deborah blood thirsty? Did Michal worry more about what people thought than God? Did Hannah deeply regret handing Samuel over to Eli? We don't know, because scripture just does not tell us their stories in full.[1]

It disappoints us that we are perpetuating the gender imbalance in a book about discipleship and leadership. However, because scripture gives a more rounded picture of the complicated male characters, with their strengths and weaknesses, they remain the focus of this book. We have included one woman towards the end, but we are sorry not to have been able to include more. Yet all that has been drawn out with each of the normal, imperfect heroes

---

1   Maybe that is a book for me to write another day with James as my co-author.

applies equally to men and women. We all have strengths and weaknesses, we all fail and get it wrong. Fallibility is not gender specific.

Liz Grier

Introduction

Christian speakers often tell tales of great heroes of the faith: men and women who, in spite of the most challenging circumstances, achieve incredible things for God. One such example is William Carey, a poverty-stricken cobbler's apprentice struggling with the death of his first child at the age of two. In the face of a general lack of interest for world mission, he set up his own missionary society and travelled to India with his family and one other man. While there, his colleague deserted him, he contracted malaria, he lost another child and his wife's mental health deteriorated to the point where she became delusional and violent. At one point she tried to kill him. Yet his faith didn't waver. Over the next twenty-eight years he and his team translated the entire Bible into India's major languages – Bengali, Oriya, Marathi, Hindi, Assamese and Sanskrit – and parts of the Bible into 209 other languages and dialects.

Another example is Jackie Pullinger, a young woman who, recently graduated from university, felt called to be a missionary. At the age of just twenty-two she bought the cheapest boat ticket to Hong Kong and went there on her own, because no missionary agency would accept her. Somehow, she managed to get a job as a music teacher in a primary school and spent her spare time walking the streets telling drug addicts and prostitutes that Jesus loved them. She's now been there for more than fifty years. Her ministry has seen God's miraculous power and provision in abundance, with hundreds of addicts set free and finding faith in Jesus.

Stories such as these are meant to encourage, but so often they can do the opposite. We are left feeling even worse about our Christian faith. We have not known illness or poverty. We have never faced such challenging circumstances. Personally speaking,

I've been ordained since an early age and have always had job and housing security. My faith has never been tested like theirs. Certainly Liz has never threatened to kill me. I think (hope?) her limit is mild disappointment!

Yet while my life looks nothing near as difficult as these amazing examples, this doesn't mean I have found faith easy. Much of the time I find it hard work. In a former job, I led a wonderful church with Liz, but we didn't always see the fruit we hoped for. I often found myself challenging and encouraging others to deal with the mess in their lives when I was struggling, and failing, to address my own. While Jackie Pullinger risked her life approaching gang members, I was simply afraid of looking weird or facing rejection. But it was no less real. Rather than comparing my achievements and challenges to Jackie's, I needed to know that there is hope for normal, broken, messed-up people like me.

For the last ten years or so I have had a mentor called Matt. I can be completely honest with him. He challenges me, my actions and my thinking, but I know that in all our conversations he has my best interests at heart. Everyone should have a mentor. Matt often surprises me with an insightful nugget of wisdom. Recently he reminded me that no one gets it right all the time. He thinks of people as being 80:20. Even the best theologians have some stuff wrong. Even the best leader isn't perfect. Society seems to focus on the 20%: the stuff that is wrong. But the amazing truth is that God is interested in the 80%. Now do not mishear me! God does not want us to turn a blind eye to the other 20% – he never turns a blind eye to sin. But he never cancels us because of it. He always offers the promise of redemption. We are called to faithfully follow Jesus, being honest in the reality of our mess rather than avoiding our brokenness and failings. Facing it can be tough: bad behaviour will bring serious consequences for some people when they address it properly. The journey back might be difficult and they will perhaps never return to ministry. But that's the minority. For most of us, God calls us to minister and lead despite our flaws.

So where can we find ordinary people stumbling along in their faith like us? Believe it or not, the Bible is full of them. The Bible introduces us to real people. The heroes of faith who weren't so heroic. Instead of heroes battling through, it tends to show us broken, messed-up people whom God used in spite of themselves. The Bible predates today's social media culture, where we all present the best bits of our lives. My reality is that we struggle to get all four of our family in the same photo without one of us looking moody or slightly odd, yet my feeds are full of perfect family videos and photos. Ironically, I've just sent Liz a photo of my Bible, computer and coffee, to show her how diligently I'm working away at this book. It's a snapshot in time of a good moment, which ignores the last ten days of procrastination.

When the Bible tells us about someone's life, we get the whole story. They were people God used in spite of all their failures and weaknesses, far more than he used them for their great strengths. They were people who can inspire us as we struggle through life seeking to follow Jesus when so easily, and so often, we find ourselves falling and failing. The Bible is full of losers who win.

In order to prevent this book from becoming longer than the Bible itself, there are huge chunks of Scripture that I gloss over or leave out. My hope is that this book will inspire you to read the stories for yourself. Unsurprisingly the Bible puts it much better than I ever will.

Having said that, are you sitting comfortably? Well, whether you are or not, we're going to begin...

Part I

THE BEGINNINGS OF LEADERSHIP

1

The father of faith

Introducing Abraham

Abraham is seen as the father of faith,[1] but what is faith? According to the Bible, 'faith is confidence in what we hope for and assurance about what we do not see' (Hebrews 11:1). Yet Abraham doesn't seem to be that much of a superstar in the faith department. When the going got tough he lied or compromised, he doubted and took things into his own hands rather than trusting in God. In fact, like most of us, he was a bit of a mixed bag.

Settling for less than God promises

Abraham's story began with his dad. (I guess that's true for most of us – when two people love each other very much they have a special cuddle and...) His dad, Terah, set out 'from Ur of the Chaldeans to go to Canaan. But when Terah and his family came to Haran, they settled there' – 400 miles away from their intended destination (Genesis 11:31). Admittedly by then they had travelled 550 miles north-west, which is plenty far enough for anyone to go without air conditioning. Interestingly, God did not explicitly call Terah to Canaan. In fact no reason at all is given for the relocation. But it was clearly God's plan for him and his family, as the rest of the story will go on to show.

How many of us set off on God's journey and settle at some point along the way? Maybe when you were young, you felt a particular

---

1 By Jews and in Scripture (cf Romans 4:16)

call from God, but it never happened. It might be that the call was to lead worship, but you never got to lead at a big event or service, so you lost heart and stopped pursuing that call. But what if the call wasn't so much about the size of the platform as your heart for worship?

I know someone who started an outreach project on an estate. At first things went well, but then as it attracted more and more people in complicated situations, it got messy. For everyone's sake it ended up becoming necessary to close the project down. That leader felt they had failed and avoided doing anything similar ever again. I know others who felt their call didn't develop and life simply crowded in. They put it on the back burner and never got around to it. This wasn't intentional; they just didn't notice their passion was reduced by the demands of work, responsibilities and family.

Like Terah, could you have settled along the way and given up on something God has called you to? I wonder what it would look like to take up that call again.

Responding to God's call

God then called Abraham, or Abram as he was known at this point, to leave the comfort of his parental home and go where he was led (Genesis 12:1–3). Abram left everything to set out into the unknown. That is faith. He obediently followed, and along the way God appeared and encouraged him.

It still doesn't seem fair to me that Abraham is credited as the 'father of faith'. What I wouldn't give for God actually to appear to me and speak so clearly. Surely that would make acting in faith easy. God has never spoken to me in the way he seemed to speak to Abraham.

Yet if I'm honest, I know that when God does speak I often miss or forget it. But Abram wasn't like me. He didn't forget. In fact, Abram set up little prompts to help him remember God's faithfulness. He built an altar each time he had a significant encounter with God (Genesis 12:7–8). Maybe I need to learn from Abram to put down markers to remember what God does for me as I journey through life. If not physical, maybe written ones, noting what God has done in my life. Journaling is usually something I resort to when the chips are down, so recording the positives is a new practice for me. But journaling is not for everyone. Our youngest son gave Liz a jam jar, or an Ebenezer jar, for Christmas. The idea is to fill it with pieces of paper on which you write the good stuff, the God moments, as they happen. Each year you start a new jar and over time you will have a collection of jars all filled with moments when you knew God at work, saw answers to prayer or recorded significant Bible verses. We are so quick to forget.

Throughout the Bible we are encouraged to remember God's good works. However we choose to do it, we need to celebrate the God moments, the good moments in our lives. These will carry us through the tough times and the challenges. Remembering that God is always faithful, and trusting in him whatever our current circumstances, is a key part of faith.

Lying: Abraham's problem with a beautiful wife

Abram was a man of God, faithfully following and meeting God, trusting him into the unknown … until there was a risk he might go hungry. Abram made it to Canaan, then encountered a famine, so he nipped off down to Egypt (Genesis 12:10).

Now, I've never experienced a famine, and for all I know it was the right thing to do, but interestingly there is no mention of God telling Abram to go to Egypt. It's far more likely he panicked and headed for somewhere that looked a safer, easier bet.

And just as we are left wondering if Abram had done the right thing, we are told about a chat that he had with his wife Sarai on the way. He told her that she was pretty gorgeous (which is a good thing to say to your wife) and that her beauty might put his life in danger (not so good). He asked her if she would mind saying (if anyone asked) that she was his sister. He hoped that if she did this, he would be treated better and would be less likely to die.

Abram and Sarai made it to Egypt and the Egyptians agreed with Abram's assessment of his wife's beauty. She obediently stuck to Abram's plan and told everyone that she was his sister. At first everything was fine. Abram did get treated better because of his deception and was given flocks and servants. But then Pharaoh began to make moves on Sarai and it started to go a bit wrong. It was necessary for God to step in to protect Sarai from Pharaoh's advances and he became ill. Pharaoh summoned Abram (personally I'd have opted for a doctor), asked what was going on and the lie was uncovered.

This 'man of faith' was not so different from us. Abram got scared, and rather than trusting God, he took matters into his own hands. He told a few lies and made a complete hash of it. How often do we sugar-coat the truth? How often are we tempted to tell a white lie or a half-truth? In my role as a leader there have been times when I haven't been totally straight with team members because I don't want to hurt their feelings. This has led to confusion, misunderstanding and hurt, which I could so easily have avoided by being honest with them. The same is true for Abram. We can see from his story that everything would have gone much more smoothly if only he'd trusted God in the first place. But he didn't.

Interestingly, this little detour made Abram very wealthy (Genesis 13:2). But we cannot 'do the math' and decide that two plus two equals four. Abram's wealth is not a sign that God condoned his lies and deception. People say that everything happens for a reason, or that God led them to act in a certain way, yet I don't think that's quite the case. When good comes out of tough situations, I think it's much more about God's grace than his orchestration, or that the ensuing good is a justification of our mistakes. Central to God's character is redemption. He can redeem anything, no matter how bad it is. Doing well in life, and prosperity, are not signs of God's approval. Rather, God has an amazing ability to bring good out of all things. 'And we know that in all things God works for the good of those who love him' (Romans 8:28).

Liz had the privilege of praying with a woman called Rebecca. She was a counsellor, and in the course of her work with abuse survivors she had become so traumatised by their stories that she herself was suffering from PTSD. She had been told over and over again by well-meaning Christians that God intended everything for good and that this would make her better at her job, more empathetic. She was left feeling scared and angry and alone. Yet as they sat and prayed, God gently showed her that he had never intended for her to be hurt or damaged by this situation. God was weeping with the victim of abuse whom Rebecca was counselling, and he was weeping with Rebecca for the harm that the abuse was now causing her. Out of God's grace and abundant love Rebecca began to be beautifully set free that day from the effects of the trauma. Her pain was never God's plan. However, we praise God that out of his glorious riches he can, and does, bring gold out of the darkest places.

Repeating patterns of behaviour

Back to Abram and now we see him return to where he was meant to be – the Negev. In his wanderings he rediscovered one of his earlier altars and again called on the name of the Lord (Genesis 13:4). Prompted by the altar, he turned his attention back to God. But, just seven chapters later, he repeated the whole sorry tale. A new place, a new king, the same old lie that Sarai was not his wife but his sister (Genesis 20:1–16). God had to intervene again, and this time he warned the king directly. When the king challenged

Abram, he said they were half-siblings. Even though there was some truth in this, it was not OK. However close to the truth your story is, it's not OK to twist it to protect yourself or deceive others.

Again, we see that Abram's wrongdoing affected others. Just as our wrongdoing will affect others. In this story it immediately affects the king and his family, but as we read on we'll see that it is a weakness played out in future generations. His son Isaac will do exactly the same thing, with the same king, in the same place, only a few chapters later (Genesis 26:6–16).

What we do, both good and bad, is easily mimicked by our children, as any parent knows! Children are a mix of their parents' genes and their parents' behaviours, both intended and otherwise. But there also seems to be a spiritual dimension to this inheritance.

Children can inherit their parents' sinful attitudes and behaviour, and this is the concept of generational sin. It is the idea that sin is passed from parent to child. In the second of the Ten Commandments there is the surprising statement that God is a jealous God and punishes children for the wrongdoing of their parents to the third and fourth generations of those who reject him. At face value it seems to say that God punishes children for their parents' sins. Yet this contradicts Ezekiel 18:20, which tells us: 'The one who sins is the one who will die. The child will not share the guilt of the parent, nor will the parent share the guilt of the child.' Also, in Jeremiah 31:29–30 it says, 'In those days people will no longer say, "The parents have eaten sour grapes, and the children's teeth are set on edge."' Therefore it can't be simply that God punishes us for the sins of our parents. Which is a relief, as repenting of our own sins is enough to deal with!

So, what is being said in the Ten Commandments? It is more that God allows us to face the impact of our parents' wrongdoing rather than that he chooses to punish us for it. There seems to be some kind of legacy resulting from the actions of previous generations. For example, a child is affected by their parent's alcoholism. Or their lying. Or their arguing. We could keep going with the list. It makes sense that there would be a spiritual inheritance just as there are emotional and genetic ones.

In the Old Testament, God's people forget about him time and time again, and choose to worship idols. In turn their children are raised in a culture that has forgotten God and worships idols and, as they grow up, it is a pattern that unsurprisingly they find themselves repeating. Similarly, if a child grows up with anger as the dominant emotion, it is their go-to response as well. We need to be alert to what we are passing on to our children and pray for ourselves and them as we discern those attributes.

But we shouldn't become paranoid or anxious about what our children inherit from us, because God's ability to bring freedom is greater than the danger of our families being enslaved. Patterns of behaviour can be broken. Being the child of an addict doesn't determine the trajectory of that child's future, even if it might make them more susceptible to addiction. God is able to create a different future for us. Interspersed with the text of the second commandment is the fact that God shows steadfast love to the thousandth generation of those who love him and keep his commandments (Deuteronomy 5:10). God wants to bless and pour out his love on the generations that are to come.

Abraham loses faith

The first time Abram met God, God promised him sons (Genesis 12:1–3). He promised that he would be a great nation and his offspring would inherit the land of Canaan. But Abram struggled to produce one son, let alone many!

After some time, Abram was fed up with great prophecies of abundance. He got into a bit of a sulk and had a good old moan at God (Genesis 15:2–4). The way things stood, if he died, everything would be inherited by Eliezer of Damascus and we don't even know who he was![2] I love the fact that in this moaning conversation Abram was being honest and real with God. He wasn't putting up a front or pretending that everything was OK. It wasn't, and he said it like it was.

God responded by telling Abram that he would indeed have his own son. A son from his body. It's just a shame God didn't unpack it a bit more and specify that it would be from his wife's body too. That would have saved a lot of trouble later.[3] God then illustrated this promise by saying that his offspring would be as numerous as the stars in the sky.

Now came Abram's moment of glory: he believed God! This was *the* moment. The moment when faith was 'credited to him as righteousness' (Genesis 15:6; Romans 4:3). Christian faith is built around this moment. Our faith, our salvation, is based on faith alone. There is nothing we can do or need to do to get right with God. We need only to believe. And Abram believed.

Don't be deceived, though. This wasn't some holy moment where he was so overwhelmed by God's presence that all doubt was gone. It wasn't like the line from that classic 80s worship song which claims that simply being in God's presence rids us of all our problems. He believed, yet he still had questions and even some doubt. The Lord still credited it to him as righteousness.

There then followed a slightly strange ritual (be prepared to skip the next bit if you're a vegetarian) involving the chopping in half of lots of animals (Genesis 15:9–21). God told Abram to bring a heifer, a goat, a ram, a dove and a pigeon. He was to cut them in half and arrange the halves in rows opposite each other with a little walkway between them. This was with the exception of the birds, which could be kept whole – I guess they were a bit small and

---

2 He was maybe a servant mentioned in Genesis 24 or the illegitimate son of a concubine. Commentators have all manner of theories, but basically we don't know!

3 Sarai took her childlessness into her own hands and offered her servant to Abram to have a child on her behalf, but then resented the fact that her plan was successful (Genesis 16).

fiddly to chop in half. This was a common practice in Abram's day. People would make a covenant by cutting animals in half. Then both parties would walk down the gap between the two halves as a binding commitment that if they broke their promise, they themselves would be cut in two.

But on this occasion, at least two odd things happen. One is that God alone made the covenant. God, by the means of a smoking firepot with a blazing torch, passed between the carcases. As I've said, normally both parties would have walked through the pieces declaring their commitment to the covenant and calling judgement on themselves if they were to break it. Yet here all the judgement was on one side. This was an unconditional covenant, with God carrying all the risk and cost. This was a foretaste of what would happen on the cross.

The second odd thing is that before the covenant was made there was a long delay in proceedings. Abram was there, the animals were there, but there was no sign of God. Everything was set and ready to go – a bit like a groom standing at the altar waiting for the bride to arrive to get married. We are left wondering if Abram is going to be jilted at the altar. Nothing happened for so long that Abram had to fight off the birds of prey trying to eat the sacrificed animals, to protect the promise.

How often do doubts come in and try to steal away our faith and the truth about God? For Abram his waiting went on so long that night came and he fell into a deep and scary sleep. It is true that God speaks, but it's still scary. It was as if this delay and darkness were representing the dark times ahead, foretold in Abram's dream, when it would feel as though God had abandoned his people and his promise altogether.

I find that one of the most quoted promises in churches is from Jeremiah: '"For I know the plans I have for you," declares the Lord, "plans to prosper you and not to harm you, plans to give you hope and a future"' (Jeremiah 29:11). What people almost never include is the fact that the previous verse says that there will be a gap of seventy years before this happens! It's given glibly as an encouragement that everything is going to be great, rather than as something to hang on to and trust in during the challenging times ahead. It was the same for Abram. The time delay that night was a hint that Abram missed, which resulted in him doubting God's promises time and again. We too doubt that God's promises will ever come true and as a result, like Abram, we end up taking things into our own hands.

About fifteen years ago Liz and I moved to Devon to start a new church to reach young people with no interest in, or connection with, faith. Before we moved, various people felt, through prayer, that it would take a long time to see any fruit. I assumed that meant about a year. Over the next few years, at every point when I felt we had achieved nothing and possibly never would, someone else would have the same prayerful revelation. I began to roll my eyes as yet another person prayed about our waiting. Yet despite our frustration at the delay, the words were a confirmation that we were headed in the right direction and should keep trusting.

Perhaps if we had seen rapid growth, and if church planting had been easy, we wouldn't have needed to keep praying and persevering. We wouldn't have had to trust God so completely, and we wouldn't have learned that it was him, and him alone, who would build his church. As it was, we learned (sometimes in the painfully hard way that is the wilderness) that we could not engineer growth or make new Christians or create a huge, successful church in our own strength. We could do nothing apart from him (John 15:5).

Taking back control

God promised Abram twice that he would be the father of a great nation, but ten years passed and all the pregnancy tests came back negative (Genesis 16:1–3). Eventually Sarai couldn't take it any more, so she came up with a cunning plan. Sadly, though, it was more foolish than cunning. In her desperation to have a baby, Sarai decided that Abram should go into baby production with her servant Hagar. Although strange to us, it was a perfectly acceptable practice in those days when servants had no rights. The servants, their possessions and even their bodies belonged entirely to their master. Hagar instantly conceived, so at least that part of the plan worked (Genesis 16:4). Yet surrogacy is never that straightforward. As soon as Hagar was pregnant, Sarai was angry with Abram and blamed him for her suffering! She was then not only not pregnant but her servant was, and on top of that her servant despised her. Or so Sarai believed.

The story seems to be all about Sarai messing up and getting it wrong, but I suggest Abram was as much to blame as she was. Have you ever wondered what Adam was up to when Eve was deceived by the serpent and took the fruit? I used to think that he was off playing with the animals or something, completely oblivious to the fall until Eve later found him and offered him a bite. But I hadn't read the Bible closely enough. 'She also gave some to her husband, who was with her' (Genesis 3:6). He stood passively by while the serpent tempted Eve.

Adam could have told the serpent to get lost. He could even have injected some truth into the conversation. But no, he just let his wife deal with the situation on her own. Even when she got it wrong and took the fruit, he could have stood firm and resisted. But he didn't. We see the same with Abram. Rather than challenge his wife's plan he just passively went along with it. Maybe he'd always been quite keen on Hagar. Maybe he was simply past hope. Maybe the plan seemed convincing. God had promised a baby from his body but hadn't specified which woman's body would bear it. We don't know what Abram thought about the plan, but we do know that he was as much to blame as Sarai. 'She/he made me do it' is not an excuse in life, just as it isn't in the playground. Abram should never have agreed to sleep with Hagar. He should have trusted God instead.

God never gives up on us

In the end Sarai treated pregnant Hagar so badly that she ran away. At this point we could expect God to pronounce some kind of judgement. I thought the Old Testament was meant to be full of wrath and judgement. Surely at this point God should have told them off and punished them. It was only fair! Instead, God declared his covenant with Abram all over again and even added to it (Genesis 17).

But even in the midst of this fresh declaration of God's covenant with Abram and promise of a child with Sarai, Abram wondered whether he should just settle for Ishmael, his illegitimate son with Hagar (Genesis 17:18). But God doesn't compromise and settle. He completely fulfils his promises in *his* way. At this point he changed Abram's name to Abraham, which means 'father of many', and Sarai's to Sarah (which is much easier to say).

This story sometimes makes me wonder if God understands anything about repentance and penance! Surely Abraham should repent and prove he's sorry before he can know God's love again. But instead of a vengeful God, needing to be appeased or grovelled to, we see a God who is like a great Dad. A Dad who picks up his son when he messes up and tells him it's all OK and he loves him.

After all this, God continued to walk with Abraham and Sarah in their moments of faith and doubt. When he sent three 'men' to tell them again of Sarah's forthcoming pregnancy she laughed at the prospect (Genesis 18:1–15). But even then, when God must have been despairing of them, he didn't say, 'I tell you what, I'll choose someone else.' No, he remained faithful, walking with Abraham and Sarah. God doesn't give up on his promises, even if we do.

Abraham's story, time and again, reveals to us a man whose heart is for the plans and purposes of God, but who struggles always to trust in him. That's very like me, like us. Abraham is described as the 'father of faith', not because his faith was rock solid but because ultimately his heart was towards God.

Jesus said that faith as small as a mustard seed can move mountains (Matthew 17:20–21). He also said that the kingdom is like a mustard seed which, although small, grows into something huge. I heard someone speak about this recently and their words totally transformed my understanding. Previously I'd focused on the smallness of the seed, but what I learned from this person was that mustard was an uncontainable weed in Jesus' day. People wouldn't plant it in the garden, because it would take over.

Abraham's faith may have faltered, but it only takes the smallest amount and it can take over and be uncontainable. God doesn't ask us to have perfect faith; he just calls us to trust him and follow him as he walks with us. If you believe that God has promised you something or given you a path to follow, and wise godly Christians agree, then don't settle, or compromise, or try to take matters into your own hands. If God's word says one thing but life's experience or people around you undermine that truth, keep believing and trusting rather than give in to the doubts. God's promises may take years to come to fruition, but they can always be trusted completely.

Abraham's ultimate faith moment

Sarah did have a son, named Isaac, and Abraham and his family settled down into living a quiet life in the land of the Philistines. Then one day God called him and he replied, 'Here I am.' The same response was given, as we will see later, by some of the great prophets like Samuel, Isaiah, and so many others. This was his ultimate call to follow God. God then told him to take the son whom he loved, and sacrifice him as a burnt offering. It made no sense. God had promised that from Isaac would come many generations. Even so, Abraham did as he was asked. God was asking Abraham to take the person he loved most in all world and give them up.

Abraham got up early the next day to do exactly that. When there are things I don't want to do, I often put them off, but Abraham obeyed immediately. Father and son travelled with their servants for three whole days. Was Isaac all excited because he was going grown-up camping with his dad? Was Abraham distraught and trying to appear fine? Eventually Abraham saw their destination in the distance and told the servants to wait behind. Then Abraham and Isaac set off alone on the final bit of the journey. Isaac carried the wood, Abraham the flint and knife. He carried the weight of them in his hand and on his heart.

Soon Isaac turned and said, 'Where is the lamb for the burnt offering?' And Abraham responded, 'God himself will provide the lamb for the burnt offering, my son' (Genesis 22:7–8). In Hebrews we read:

> By faith Abraham, when God tested him, offered Isaac as a sacrifice. He who had embraced the promises was about to sacrifice his one and only son, even though God had said to him, 'It is through Isaac that your offspring will be reckoned.' Abraham reasoned that God could even raise the dead, so in a manner of speaking, he did receive Isaac back from death.
> (Hebrews 11:17–19)

Even if he had faith that Isaac would be OK, he still had to place Isaac on the altar and tie him up. We have no idea what that must have been like for them both. Abraham raised the knife over his son ready to strike, when the angel of the Lord called out to him. This time, he said his name twice, maybe with a hint of urgency, and Abraham replied as he had before, 'Here I am.' To which the angel responded, 'Do not lay a hand on the boy ... Do not do anything to him. Now I know that you fear God, because you have not withheld from me your son, your only son.'

At that moment, Abraham spotted a ram behind him, caught in a bush, and sacrificed that instead of his son. He named the place Jehovah Jireh, 'The LORD Will Provide'. God then reasserted his blessing over Abraham and his descendants. Abraham and Isaac collected the servants and they headed off back to Beersheba. I simply cannot imagine what they talked about on the way home.

The account of Abraham being asked to sacrifice Isaac starts by saying that God tested Abraham. It ends by saying that he knew Abraham feared him. But it can't just be about God testing him, because God already knew Abraham. Therefore, this testing had to be for Abraham's sake rather than God's. God would never have harmed the child, but Abraham had to demonstrate trust and learn through what happened.

Before we reflect further, we do need to address the elephant in the room: how could God do that to someone? Years ago, I met up with one of the teachers who'd inspired me most at school and whom I kept in touch with over the years. Our conversation turned to faith. I was so excited as we'd never managed to talk about faith before. But then he said, 'I could never believe in the kind of abusive God who tells one of his followers to sacrifice their child to him.' I can't remember how I responded. I probably garbled something about God never intending to make Abraham go through with it. But that answer is insufficient. Even if it was the case, it still didn't make it OK!

The killing of children is abhorrent. It is offensive to us in our modern context, and so it should be. But we need to remember that the culture and context Abraham was living in were very different. Child sacrifice was common, and the fact that it was not part of the practice of the followers of Yahweh was hugely significant. God's people were always meant to be a light to other nations and faiths, showing them a better way to live. The significance of this incident lies in what it points to. It demonstrates Abraham's faith, as the father of faith, but it also points to the heart of Christian faith: the cross.

Abraham's call to sacrifice his son, which is atrocious to us, points to God's willingness to sacrifice his Son for us. Abraham told his son, 'God himself will provide the lamb for the burnt offering.' Jesus was later called the Lamb of God.

The hill where this all happened is likely to have been the hill up which, so much later, God's own Son would carry wood for his sacrifice. This story of a father willing to sacrifice his son whom he loved points to a far greater story of a Father willing to sacrifice his one and only Son whom he loved, out of his immeasurable love for us. It also lays before us a challenge and test for our faith. What are we unwilling to lay down before God? He won't ever ask us to sacrifice a child or spouse, literally or figuratively, but he may ask whether we are willing to obey him over them. For all of us, there are things that have a greater hold over our lives than God. Do we have the faith and trust to give them to God?

I once heard this helpful illustration:

Once upon a time, there was a man whose pride and joy was a huge bunch of balloons. One day, he won a trip on a luxurious cruise ship: an all-expenses-paid extravaganza. Upon boarding, he eagerly explored the decks, relishing the hors d'oeuvres table and the swimming pool. However, he quickly realised that his beloved balloons were too large to fit through any of the ship's doors or hallways. He couldn't even reach the dining room or his cabin.

To keep his balloons, he decided to stay on deck, sleeping in a lounge chair by the pool and surviving on the tiny hors d'oeuvres. The dining room's aromas grew more tantalising each day, and while the lounge chair was delightful on the first starry night, his back soon ached, and the bugs became unbearable.

After nearly two weeks of enduring this hardship, he could take it no longer. He bid farewell to his precious balloons and timidly stepped into the hallway.

To his astonishment, he discovered a stunning dining room at the end of the hall, filled with every type of food imaginable, all cooked to perfection. That evening, he was shown to his cabin, which featured an unimaginably soft bed, fresh towels, blankets and everything needed for a cosy stay.

He couldn't believe how much time he had wasted clinging to his cherished balloons when he could've been enjoying all of this the whole time.

As we have seen, Abraham tried to trust God but all too often ended up attempting to sort things out for himself. His failure to trust, for example with Hagar, or his lies around his relationship with Sarah, caused unnecessary hurt and pain. Abraham had to learn to be obedient and trust in God's promises. Through Abraham, God was founding a new nation – one that would know God and trust God and be faithful to him.

The people of God would need to learn, time and again, to trust and obey God, just as we need to keep on learning today. How often do we sing in church and declare that we will trust God fully, but then, as soon as pressure comes, we trust in the ways of the world or our own understanding? How often, when it feels as though God's promises are slow in being fulfilled, do we give up and settle with where we are or take things into our own hands? Are we willing to put our confidence in what we hope for and trust in what we do not see? Are we going to be people of faith, however shaky that faith might be at times?

2

The hustler

Introduction

Jacob's life is a tale of self-centredness and rivalry. Even before he was born, he was out for himself. Yet God still met with him. God made promises to him that he didn't deserve and blessed him in unfathomable ways. His prosperity was not down to his scheming and cheating, but rather down to God's love and generosity.

Sibling rivalry

Sibling rivalry started in the womb for twins Jacob and Esau, Isaac's sons and Abraham's grandsons. In fact, there was so much kicking during her pregnancy that their mum, Rebekah, desperately asked God what was going on (Genesis 25:22–23). He responded that she had two nations within her and that the older would serve the younger. Then they came out fighting. Esau was born first, with Jacob following hot on his heels, literally grasping Esau's heel, trying to win the race. Esau came out as hairy as a rug. In fact, the name Esau means 'hairy', so no points for imaginative naming there! Jacob means 'heel grasper', which is a Hebrew idiom for 'deceiver'. Well, it couldn't have been more prophetic. Grasping and deceiving became his *modus operandi*.

As they grew up, Esau was a bit of a lad, often out hunting and killing things, whereas Jacob was a home boy. This meant that he got to spend lots of time with his mum and was her favourite – a mummy's boy. Esau, on the other hand, was his dad's favourite (Genesis 25:28). He probably worked his way into his dad's heart through his stomach and passion for wild game. As they got older, the family division became worse. From the outset Jacob wanted to be favourite. He wanted what wasn't his and he was willing to hustle to get it.

I have an older sister. As children we got on well, but we knew how to wind each other up in an instant. If you have brothers or sisters, you will be able to relate to this. On one memorable holiday we stayed in a place by a river. We were deemed old enough and trustworthy enough to be allowed out on our own in a little motorboat. The adventure! The independence! It was so exciting … for a while.

I don't know what my sister said, and I certainly can't remember what I said, but one day on that holiday we had a big argument. I was so upset, I couldn't stand to be in the same place as her, let alone the same boat, for a moment longer. I stood up, jumped into the river and swam to shore. I remember that we got into trouble later. I felt very hard done by; my sister had not only upset me, but she also got me into trouble! However, I'm delighted to report that her day ended worse than mine. We were sharing a room with bunkbeds and I was on the top bunk (result!). In the night, I was sick. Very sick. All over the bottom bunk and my poor sister.

Lots of sibling rivalry is about our worth. Are they better than me? Who's the favourite? Equally, it can be about wanting to get our own way. Brothers and sisters are in our space – they mean we have to share. And with them we can dispense with the social filters. If I make my friend cry I risk losing the friendship, but my brother or sister isn't going anywhere. The people we should be able to be most ourselves with can be left with the worst of us. Sibling rivalry is about looking to our own interests and not caring about the other person. It's selfish and damaging, and no one wins.

Developing patterns of behaviour

The Bible tells us that one day Esau came home exhausted from a day out chasing and killing things, and he was starving (Genesis

25:29–34). He wanted food *now*. In the absence of microwave meals, Jacob, never one to miss a trick, offered his stew for the exorbitant cost of Esau's rights and privileges as the firstborn son. Like any teenage lad, Esau's brain was wired to focus on 'now' rather than 'later'.[1] Add to that a touch of drama and he declared that if he didn't get food immediately he was going to die. Who cared about the future and birthrights when he wasn't going to be alive to enjoy them? So Jacob gave him his meat stew and got Esau's birthright in return.

Esau wanted his immediate needs satisfied with no regard for the future. How often do we choose instant gratification over the long term? It fits the buy-now-pay-later world we live in. You may feel that Jacob hardly did anything wrong. Hebrews 12:16 goes as far as to describe Esau as godless for selling his birthright for a meal. Jacob clearly knew what he was up to. Jacob chose to exploit the situation.

Any behaviour can grow into a habit. If something works for us, we're likely to repeat it. Our moral compass can drift further and further from true north, or simply from truth. With drugs, alcohol, food, or whatever it is, people need greater and greater amounts to satisfy the craving or to get the same buzz. The same is true here. A spur-of-the-moment decision to play the advantage and exploit his brother would become Jacob's default. The deceiver was on the path of deception. Combine this with a pushy mum who wanted every blessing for her precious boy, and the stage was set for the big con …

The pattern continues

As Isaac came to the end of his life, he wanted to die a happy man. He asked Esau for a last bowl of his amazing fresh game stew (Genesis 27:1–4). So Esau went to find the finest game. But catching

---

1 The pre-frontal cortex is the part of the brain that helps encourage focus and delayed gratification. Its main development and growth takes place during adolescence.

the finest game takes time. Enough time for Mum to see her chance. Rebekah told Jacob to kill one of the flock and she would cook it. Then he could pretend he was Esau and get his blessing.

So, after raiding the dressing-up box, Jacob hustled his dad (Genesis 27:15–40). He wore Esau's clothes and some animal hair to pretend to be Esau, and conned his dad into giving him the blessing for the firstborn son. As with all lies, it wasn't a foolproof plan because, when Esau eventually appeared with his venison pie, all was discovered.

Esau was so angry, he wanted to kill his brother. This was a particular problem for Jacob since we know that Esau was a hunter, and Jacob had spent his youth hanging out in the kitchen. Their mum recognised that this may not go her favourite's way and so tricked Isaac into sending Jacob off to her brother's place to keep him safe.

Do you notice that Rebekah was possibly even more manipulative and deceptive than Jacob? As we will soon discover, her brother Laban was just as bad. As we will also see, Rebekah's other character flaw of favouritism would be a real problem with Jacob. Rebekah was the protagonist and even told Jacob that the blame was on her (Genesis 27:13). But Jacob was still guilty.

As we saw with Abraham, bad traits can be passed down from one generation to the next. We see it time and time again in the lives of Bible characters. We also see it in our own lives. I meet a lot of people whose parents haven't been the best and whose failures have set their child down an unhelpful path. Sometimes we learn behaviour and coping mechanisms just to survive in difficult circumstances, but we are still responsible for our own actions.

If we want to break a pattern of behaviour, first we need to acknowledge it and own it. As with alcoholics, the first step is to admit there is a problem. That is easier said than done, since we prefer to blame others rather than take personal responsibility. But we need to repent, or turn our back, on our poor behaviours.

Several years ago, I came across a helpful model for repentance.[2] It's not a formula, but simply breaks down the concept of repentance and helps people go deeper in prayer. It's based on five 'R's:

- *Recognise*: There's something that's not OK, which I need to own. It may be someone else's fault that I started thinking or acting in this way, but I'm responsible for continuing to do so.
- *Renounce*: I turn my back on believing a lie, holding on to an attitude or acting in a particular way.
- *Receive*: I take a moment to receive God's forgiveness for myself or forgive someone else for what they did, how it made me feel and what it made me believe about myself, or God, or others.
- *Rebuke*: I pray for release from any spiritual influence or hold in this area of my life, now that I've repented.
- *Replace*: I ask God to show his truth to replace the lies I have been believing, or what it looks like to live differently in repentance. For example, I may feel unlovable. This is a lie. Scripture clearly states that God loves every single person he has created.[3] So if God loves everyone, then that includes me. I too am lovable. But somehow this truth needs to be turned from head knowledge into something that changes my heart, how I feel and what I believe about myself. Replacing, in this example, may be allowing God to bring to mind a memory of someone doing something that demonstrates I'm actually lovable. God needs to speak to our hearts with a language we will understand, so he will speak differently to each of us.

---

2 Jesus Ministry conference in 2004: 'Freedom & Renewal for Christians & Churches'.

3 Where do we even start with this truth? Well, try reading Zephaniah 3:17; John 3:16 and 1 John 4:10, and if that isn't enough to convince you, then do a quick Google search and see how many Bible verses you can turn up.

Owning his sin

Jacob fled for his life (Genesis 27:41 – 28:5). He knew that if Esau did catch him, he would be unlikely to come out of the encounter well. He was terrified. He got as far as he could before dark (Genesis 28:10–22). Exhausted from the journey, and afraid, he pulled up a stone as a pillow and lay down to sleep. (Serious respect! Liz has started taking her pillow from home when we go away, in case where we're staying doesn't have the right type of pillows!) As he slept, he began to dream. And this was no ordinary dream. In it, God himself spoke to Jacob. He made very similar promises to those he gave Abraham about land and descendants.[4] God also promised, 'I am with you and will watch over you wherever you go... I will not leave you until I have done what I have promised you' (Genesis 28:15).

Jacob was understandably stunned. He used his pillow to make a pillar (Liz couldn't do that) and called the place Bethel, which means 'house of God'. He declared that if God did what he promised, then 'the LORD will be my God' (Genesis 28:21). He also offered to tithe all he earned – and that was before ever hearing a sermon on giving![5]

I shared Jacob's story with some young people and asked them what they would have expected God to say to Jacob in his dream. One girl said, 'You're an idiot' (only she didn't put it quite so politely). But she was totally right. He'd tricked and deceived his way through life and was running for his life. He'd messed everything up. In the previous section I talked about repentance. I would have expected God to tell him to go back, make amends and say sorry. But, bizarrely, God did nothing of the sort. Jacob, up to this point, had cheated and conned his way through life, but rather

---

4   Quick bit of Bible trivia: the land Jacob was lying on, which God promised to him, was exactly the place God had called Abraham to leave in the beginning.

5   Tithing is the biblical, and now Christian, principle of giving 10% of what we earn, or are given, back to God.

than telling him off God made amazing promises to him. Jacob responded by declaring that he would follow God.

Surely that wasn't fair! Shouldn't he at least have been told off and disciplined? It wasn't OK! Well, unless I'd been in his shoes. In which case it would have been very OK. Here, however, God acted in a way that is very different from how many of us perceive him, or church, to be. Most people expect faith in God and going to church to be all about telling people off. In fact, while taking sin very seriously, God and his Church are all about grace and forgiveness. We mess up and muddle through life, hurting ourselves and others. But God, instead of punishing us as we deserve, comes in the person of his Son and dies for us. He promises us life now and in eternity. He promises he will be with us by living in us by his Holy Spirit. That's not fair. But it's definitely OK, and it's definitely amazing.

I love Bono's reflection on the concept of grace:[6]

Grace defies reason and logic. Love interrupts, if you like, the consequences of your actions, which in my case is very good news indeed, because I've done a lot of stupid stuff. But I'd be in big trouble if karma was going to finally be my judge. I'd be in deep s***. It doesn't excuse my mistakes, but I'm holding out for grace. I'm holding out that Jesus took my sins onto the cross, because I know who I am, and I hope I don't have to depend on my own religiosity.[7]

The tables turn on Jacob

Jacob journeyed on. He found the home of his uncle Laban and very romantically fell hopelessly in love with Laban's daughter, his

---

6 In fact, I love Bono. I'm a bit of a fanboy for U2 – something for which my family consistently mock me.

7 Michka Assayas, *Bono: In Conversation with Michka Assayas* (New York: Riverhead, 2005).

cousin Rachel. It was love at first sight, with a flock of sheep looking on. He helped her get water from the well and then they kissed (Genesis 29:11). So it might just have been a cousinly greeting, but it could have been deeply romantic and sweet (or, as my boys would say, 'gross'). We don't know. But we do know that Jacob went to his uncle's house and hung around the place like some lovesick teenager.

Eventually Laban said, 'If you're going to hang around helping out for any longer, I guess we'd better start paying you' (see Genesis 29:15). Jacob said he'd work for free for seven years in return for marrying Rachel. He worked the seven years and 'they seemed like only a few days to him because of his love for her' (Genesis 29:20). This is more like a Jane Austen novel than the Bible![8]

Although it felt like only a few days, as soon as the time was up, he demanded his bride and the wedding celebrations began. There was a big feast and that night Jacob went to bed with his beloved bride. In the morning, he rolled over to revel in the delight of seeing his beautiful bride first thing in the morning (he was new to this marriage thing). To his horror, he wiped the sleep from his eyes and discovered he'd got the wrong bride! The new wife in his bed was not his beloved Rachel but her older, and less attractive, sister Leah. The conner had been conned.

I'm not entirely sure how you can spend the night with the wrong sister and not notice. I know this was pre-electricity, but still … Cunning Uncle Laban suggested that he marry Rachel too but wangled another seven years of labour from Jacob for the privilege (although this time he could marry her first and work the seven years afterwards).

Up until this point Jacob had only been concerned about himself. Now the shoe was on the other foot. It's so easy for us to see life through the lens of our feelings and needs. For example, we can

---

8   In the spirit of honesty, I've never actually read a Jane Austen novel, but Liz has. Well, I think she has. She's definitely watched all the films!

convince ourselves that when we are economical with the truth, it's for a good reason and understandable. However, if someone else does the same thing to us, we see it as deceiving and dishonourable.

When someone wrongs us it's easy to get so caught up in our own hurt that we fail to have any compassion or concern for them. When driving, I am often disappointed in other people's lane discipline or poor use of indicators. Yet when I'm daydreaming in the middle lane, I can reason with myself that my driving is excusable.

A while ago, I was impatiently battling with bad traffic and got cross when someone cut in front of me. One of our sons retorted that I needed to be more like Desmond Tutu. Tutu said that we can either get frustrated, or imagine that the other driver's wife might have pancreatic cancer and show them grace and tolerance.[9] Ever since, if I exhibit any hint of impatience at another driver, one of the family will say, 'His wife may have pancreatic cancer.' I haven't stopped getting impatient with other drivers, but I do try to remember that I don't know what troubles and stresses they are facing in their lives, and that their bad driving is not all about me!

Desperate to be loved

Jacob found himself with not one wife but two. Here began a whole new catalogue of issues of rivalry and favouritism. Quickly Leah began to have children. In the naming of her children, we get to understand something of Leah's struggles. She clearly knew she was the unwanted bride, the unwelcome gift. Yet she continued to hope that having children would cause her husband to have some affection for her.

She called her firstborn Reuben, saying it was 'because the LORD has seen my misery. Surely my husband will love me now' (Genesis

---

9 His Holiness the Dalai Lama and Archbishop Desmond Tutu with Douglas Abrams, *The Book of Joy: Lasting Happiness in a Changing World* (New York: Avery Publishing Group, 2016), p. 136.

29:32). Reuben means 'See! A son'. It's as if she was saying, 'I'm the real wife! Now notice me!' After the birth of her next child she said, 'Because the LORD heard that I am not loved, he gave me this one too' (verse 33). She named him Simeon, which means 'one who hears'. Then came Levi and she said, 'Now at last my husband will become attached to me' (verse 34).[10] Only Leah's fourth child carried a sense of happiness. When Judah was born, she said, 'This time I will praise the LORD' (verse 35).[11]

In the meantime, Rachel hadn't been able to have any children. Even though she knew how much her husband loved her, her measured response was, 'Give me children, or I'll die!' (Genesis 30:1). In fact she was so desperate that she went for the old family trick – or should I say mistake? She told her husband to sleep with her maidservant, Bilhah, so that she could have children for her. And Bilhah indeed got pregnant and bore a son. The poor lad was named according to what his birth did for his mum, or rather his mum's owner. He was called Dan, which means 'he has vindicated', because Rachel believed God had vindicated her. Again, Bilhah got pregnant. Along came Naphtali, which means 'struggle', because she said, 'I have had a great struggle with my sister and I have won' (Genesis 30:8). How many of us have won battles in life, and in the process lost the war? We can get so caught up in the fight that we lose all sense of perspective.

This fight certainly wasn't over and it took another strange turn. Leah stopped getting pregnant and decided that what was good for one was good for the other, so offered her husband her slave, Zilpah. Zilpah gave birth to Gad, meaning 'good fortune', and then Asher, meaning 'happy'. Leah was, at last, happy and believed that women would call her happy as a result. What a dangerous way of finding happiness.

---

10 Levi sounds like 'attached'.

11 Judah sounds like the Hebrew for 'praise'.

Then things got even stranger. One day Reuben brought home some mandrakes for his mum Leah. Rachel wanted some of them. Leah responded, 'Wasn't it enough that you took away my husband? Will you take my son's mandrakes too?' Just this phrase speaks volumes about the state their relationship was in. In response Rachel offered Leah a night with Jacob in exchange for the plant roots (Genesis 30:14ff.). All because she believed that mandrakes would increase her fertility. How devastated Rachel must have been when she later discovered that the night of traded sex resulted in another pregnancy for Leah.

This time Issachar, meaning 'reward', was born. His name implies that she saw the child as a reward from God for giving her servant to Jacob to produce children. But this cannot be true. God wouldn't have rewarded her action. God commanded marriage to take place between one man and one woman and for children to be a fruit of that marriage. He did not include in the marriage as many servants as you fancy. Quite apart from any understanding of what marriage is, it is an appalling way to treat a servant. It is sexual slavery and would never be God's intention.

Sometimes people are confused by the Old Testament, wrongly understanding that poor behaviour is approved or instigated by God because it's not challenged or corrected by him. We can easily imagine that if something is written in Scripture, it is part of God's approved will. But we need to be alert to the fact that just because things happen without a divine corrective, or Old Testament characters attribute them to God, this does not mean that their thinking is always theologically accurate.[12] Just like us they sometimes got it wrong.

Leah went on to have a final son, Zebulun. Unusually, Scripture goes on to say that Leah later gave birth to a daughter, whom

---

12 Admittedly, it is very strange that God does seem to intervene at certain points in the account. In 29:31 it says, 'When the LORD saw that Leah was not loved, he enabled her to conceive, but Rachel remained childless.' In 30:17 it says, 'God listened to Leah, and she became pregnant,' and later in 30:22, 'Then God remembered Rachel; he listened to her and enabled her to conceive.'

she named Dinah. No other daughter is mentioned in this whole complicated episode. Sadly, it is likely that she is only mentioned because later she will be raped and her brothers will wipe out a whole town's menfolk in revenge.

Even to the end, Leah hoped that her children would change her relationship with her husband, since Zebulun's name means 'honour' and she hoped that Jacob would treat her with honour. Leah's hopes are not so strange. A while ago a member of our team talked to a teenage girl who was confused after having had sex with a lad. Her expectation was that this would make him feel more for her and create a greater attachment. In practice it did nothing of the sort. He'd got what he wanted and was less interested rather than more. How many people have had sex, or even married someone, to make the person love them or so they can feel loved?

It also speaks of how easily any of us can feel unwanted or unloved. Rachel was the love of Jacob's life, yet this wasn't enough and she became jealous of her sister. The fact that Leah had given Jacob babies, and Rachel hadn't, became all-consuming to the point where she said that if she didn't have a baby she would die. Then in her desperation she offered Jacob her servant to reproduce with. Had she learned nothing from her husband's grandparents?

Our sense of whether we are loved or not isn't rational. When I was a young curate in my early twenties, there was a formidable clergy widow who came to the church. On several occasions she came to me distressed, asking what she'd done wrong. I had no idea what she was talking about. She would then say that I'd blanked her or glared at her as I processed out at the end of the service. The truth was, by the time I'd got to the back of the church, my mind was focused solely upon grabbing a coffee before going to talk to people. I wasn't thinking about her at all – my mind was miles away. Yet here was a lady in her eighties worrying about what a young curate thought about her.

At the heart of the Christian faith is God's abundant, unchanging love for us. If God loves us, we can have total security and confidence regardless of what other people feel about us. One of my favourite school assembly illustrations that I give involves a sponge and a bowl of water. I take the dry sponge and talk about how sponges love water. They will soak it all up. Then I act as if the sponge is hunting for water and consuming the drops of water I spilled on the way in. If we don't feel very loved, we can be like that. We are desperate for any love we can find, and will soak it up. Whereas if you soak a sponge in water, it doesn't need any more. In fact, it has loads to give away. At which point I swing it around and get as many pupils as I can wet. When we know we are loved – when we are soaked in God's love, rather than looking for love – we can in turn pour out love to others.

Back to Jacob. Rachel, the only woman he really loved, eventually got pregnant. She gave birth to a son, Joseph, who instantly became the favourite. He got all the best presents, wasn't made to do any chores, and as a result this blended family of stepbrothers hated him. But that's a whole other story, which we will come to a bit later.

Jacob seems to have been pretty passive in the whole process of having a family. At a time of clear patriarchy, when women had little power and few rights, it reads as if Jacob simply went along with the actions of his wives. He never intervened or spoke up, other than in one moment of defensiveness when Rachel declared that if he didn't give her children she would die. He got angry with her and lashed out, saying, 'Am I in the place of God, who has kept you from having children?' (Genesis 30:2). I wonder how much pain could have been avoided if he had spoken up. But he apparently did nothing and simply carried on working for his father-in-law, who also did nothing to interfere with his daughters' quarrels.

Facing up

Much later, Jacob set out to resolve his messy relationship with Esau (Genesis chapters 32–33). It can't have been an easy decision to go back, because when Jacob left home, Esau was all set to kill him. Yet Jacob headed off to meet Esau again. When he got close, he sent messengers to arrange a meeting. Soon he learned that Esau was on his way to meet him with 400 men! He was terrified and started to prepare. He split his family and possessions in two so that he wouldn't lose everything in one go, and then started organising a gift for his brother of hundreds of goats, sheep, donkeys and so on. He sent them in groups with carefully briefed servants to tell Esau that the abundance of livestock was a gift for him. The hope was that, by the time Esau actually got to Jacob, all his anger would have been softened by such overwhelming generosity.

But Jacob was still worried about meeting with Esau and spent a long night on his own awaiting the fateful encounter. He had already prayed to God in desperation, but that night he met with God in a far more profound way. A 'man' appeared and wrestled with him until dawn. Before he left, Jacob asked him for a blessing. The 'man' asked Jacob his name. In effect, he was asking Jacob not only to give his name but to own what he was. As soon as he confessed his name, the 'man' said, 'Your name will no longer be Jacob, but Israel' (Genesis 32:28). In other words, 'deceiver' would no longer be his identity. His new name was about so much more than him as an individual; it would be the identity of a nation: God's people. Israel means 'struggles with God'. It speaks of struggling against God, as Israel (the man and the nation) would consistently. It also talks about an engagement and proximity of relationship with God.

Israel described his night-time encounter as seeing God 'face to face'. God chose Israel, a man who had nothing to commend him, who had done nothing to earn God's love. How similar is that to us? God chooses us when we have done nothing to deserve it. In fact, Jacob had done a lot to warrant God turning away from him and giving up on him, and yet God did the opposite. He challenged him to face up to who he was, his actions and identity, and then restored to him a new future. And God offers us the same. But we must be willing to own our sin and brokenness. The challenge for us is to believe that God will accept us if we humble ourselves and seek his face.

In my experience, a lot of people expend huge amounts of energy trying to bury and avoid the stuff that hurts. Ultimately this is exhausting and futile. For many of us, the first step of healing is to face the mess. We must acknowledge the lies it has left us believing about ourselves and recognise the labels we carry around, revealing how we truly view ourselves.[13] Because until we name them and expose them for the lies they are, God can't give us truth to replace them.

Often, in the process of acknowledging the past, God will allow these difficult and painful memories to resurface. God wants to take us back there, not to hurt us, but so that he can bring love and healing in place of the shame we are left carrying. Often we can feel we are to blame or deserved what happened, whereas God wants to show us a whole different perspective.

We have been privileged to walk alongside many who were courageous enough to trust God with their innermost thoughts and fears. And what we have seen, time and again, is that God acts gently and kindly. He will never force us to go where we are not willing to go, and he will move at our speed and pace. He is a God who longs to redeem and restore the past; who longs to give us a future; who longs for us to live a life with him in freedom.

Israel, the man God called to be the basis of the whole story of his people, had no real redeeming features and yet he was the one God transformed to become the 'father' of his people. That has to inspire hope in you and me, no matter what we think or feel about ourselves. It doesn't matter how much we have failed and messed up – there is still hope.

---

13 For some examples from people I've prayed with: 'I'm unlovable', 'I'm worthless', 'I have no value' or 'I have to be successful to be lovable', 'I have to be perfect', 'I have to be in control', 'It's too late; I've messed up too badly' …

Jacob's story is not one of instant transformation. In fact, his faith had its ups and downs from his first encounter with God in a dream to the night he wrestled and beyond. It is no overnight conversion story. It's not miraculous. His whole life he would continue to struggle with favouritism and the behaviour of his children, just as his parents did before him. But God would always be central to his story.

3

Favourite child

Introduction

Often people who don't know much about the Bible will still know something about Joseph. This is probably due in part to Andrew Lloyd Webber. It's just a shame that the refrain of his musical totally misses the point. I'm sorry to break it to you, but any dream won't do! The dreams in Joseph's life are only significant because they were given by God, and were not any old dreams. Throughout Joseph's life he constantly made mistakes. But comfortingly, God was always at work, using those mistakes for Joseph's good. It's a wonderful tale of redemption.

Parental pressure and favouritism

As we've already learned, Israel (Jacob) had twelve sons and one daughter (that we hear of) by four different women. In a family with four mums, the sibling rivalry must have been off the scale. Especially when it became clear that Joseph was their dad's undisputed favourite child (Genesis 37:3–35).

The first thing we hear about Joseph is that he was tending the flocks with some of his half-brothers, the sons of the maidservants. Leah's boys were obviously elsewhere. There was already a distinct divide between the children. The next time we hear about Joseph is when he told tales to his dad about his half-brothers' behaviour. He was the favourite kid and he was a sneak.

To add fuel to the fire, he was then bought a special ornamental coat by his dad. Some have described it as 'technicolor'. It certainly wasn't one that would be worn for physical labour. It was a sign of honour and status.

Things got worse when he shared his dreams with them; dreams in which his brothers bowed down to him. You've got to wonder if this kid had any self-awareness at all. He was so in love with himself, and immersed in his dad's love, that he didn't consider the effect of his behaviour on his siblings. And they hated him.

One fateful day he donned his special coat and graced them with his presence. Their dad had sent him to check on how they were. So Joseph swanned around while his brothers slaved away on the farm. They saw him in the distance, strutting towards them, his coat flapping behind him, and decided enough was enough. It was time to deal with the dreamer once and for all.

They plotted to kill him and throw his body in a pit. They planned to say that an animal had eaten him. Undoubtedly, they would have done this if Reuben hadn't intervened, suggesting that they avoid bloodshed and just throw Joseph in a pit without the killing bit. He intended to rescue Joseph later and return him to his dad (Genesis 37:21). But without Reuben realising, Judah saw an opportunity when some traders passed by, and suggested to the other brothers that they sell him rather than kill him. They retrieved Joseph from the pit and sold him into slavery. This is where Joseph's incredible journey of disaster and restoration began.

It's really easy as a parent to project our fears and needs on to our children. This is most blatant in the world of celebrities. The media often tells tales of children pressurised or exploited by their parents' ambition. Recent examples include Britney Spears, Zac Efron, Andre Agassi and Tiger Woods. Pressure is not always all bad. Many other celebrities put their success down to their parents' encouragement and even pushing. We see this in the film *King Richard*, which tells the story of Venus and Serena Williams' dad. Meanwhile the opposite is true: if your parents aren't interested in encouraging things like sport or music, it's far less likely that you'll excel in them.

I think Liz and I are the perfect counter-balance to each other's attitudes to studying. Liz always had the ability to do brilliantly and so worked to achieve the best she could. I knew I was never going to get top marks, so I did what needed to be done, giving me more time for serving God, enjoying university life and having fun. We've recently discovered that for one of our sons our combination of approaches led him to feel pressured to achieve academically *and* enjoy all the extras at the same time. This eventually became an intolerable burden. Neither of us realised what we were placing on his shoulders.

Rob Parsons, from Care for the Family, referenced the old saying 'Parenting is 50% fear and 50% guilt' in his Spring 2024 letter to supporters. He added: 'I sometimes think that definition is a little light on the guilt side!' I relate to this a lot, but I'm mindful that we need to be aware of when we are projecting our hopes, fears and disappointments on to our children and do our best to stop. What we can do is be there to support them through their challenges. We should try not to push them towards what we might do in similar circumstances but help them find their own way through.

A young person can have all the love imaginable and yet, rather than find confidence in it and generously share that love with others, become egotistical and self-absorbed. Joseph had no need to compete with his brothers – he had won before they even started – and yet he did compete. Admittedly, it may not have been that simple. By this time Rachel, his mum, had died giving birth to his brother Benjamin. It's entirely possible that Jacob initially struggled to love the young baby whose birth had resulted in the death of his beloved wife. Perhaps, in Jacob's grief, Joseph became the sole focus of his feelings for the woman he had loved most. Jacob poured attention on Joseph and was so fearful of losing him that he didn't send him out to work with his brothers.

Maybe Joseph shared his dreams with his brothers to make them see that he was special in a bid to stop them treating him as a nobody, or maybe it was just to help him feel better about himself. Whatever the reasons for his actions, instead of feeling secure in the love of his father, he struggled and competed with his brothers. It's easy for us to try to find love through others or by comparing ourselves to others, but it will never work and will end in disappointment and hurt.

Finding integrity

Joseph's early life was certainly complicated, and significantly, in all the mess and confusion, God is not mentioned. The traders took Joseph with them into Egypt and it wasn't until he arrived there that we are told the Lord was with him (Genesis 39). Suddenly the story takes on an extra dimension. His life was no longer all about him.

During his time in Egypt, Jacob was quickly recognised for serving his master Potiphar well. But sadly he wasn't just noticed for his work ethic, as he caught the attention of Potiphar's wife. She relentlessly pursued the young man day after day, trying to seduce him. Joseph steadfastly resisted, not necessarily because he wasn't interested, but because he knew that to succumb to her advances would be a sin against God. During one particularly passionate request, he was forced to flee from the house, leaving Potiphar's wife clinging on to his cloak. Furious at being turned down, and left with the coat that could be used as incriminating evidence, she had Joseph arrested and he was thrown in prison.

Once again, people in the prison began to notice Joseph and particularly his talents in interpreting dreams (Genesis 40). But Joseph seems to have undergone some character development since the days with his family, as he entirely credited God for the skill (Genesis 41:16). Life for him was no longer all about trying to find love and self-worth by making himself feel better than others. So great was his transformation that even when it must have felt to him as if the bottom was falling out of his world, he stayed faithful and close to God.

Something happened to turn Joseph from a spoiled brat into a man of great integrity. Outwardly his circumstances looked desperate. He was a slave in a foreign land. His family had gone beyond rejecting him and sold him into slavery. When a woman offered her body to him, he didn't think about the optics of the situation in his refusal, but about what God wanted him to do.

Is that our motivation? If we are honest, are there times when our behaviour is motivated by what others would think rather than by integrity? The other day we were out as a family and just as I stepped on to a pedestrian crossing, a car sped across it. I angrily flapped my arms at the driver, trying to educate him in the Highway Code. But Liz kindly suggested that I might want to rethink my fury, particularly as I was wearing my bishop's regalia. On reflection, having got past my immense gratitude to my wife, I wondered what concerned me most: my actions or how my actions might have appeared as a representative of the Church. I like to think that I act the same whatever I am wearing, but there are occasions when I realise that I am more concerned about appearances than I'd like to admit.

I've always been uncomfortable about the concept of having separate professional and personal social media accounts. I realise that there can be value in having two, in terms of boundaries and what it's appropriate to share in a professional context. But I worry there is a danger that we can live two lives. God calls us to be the same person wherever we are. I was shocked to discover many young people and students in our church had two social media accounts: an open one for parents, future employers and so on, and a hidden one. Also, on too many occasions at our previous church, I would join a conversation only for someone to fall silent halfway through an anecdote. I'd ask what they were talking about and they would say that it was better not to share it, because I wouldn't approve. This made me sad, because the question should never have been whether I would approve, but whether God would approve. God isn't a killjoy, but we should seek always to live by his standards, whether our actions are seen or unseen.

Paul's letter to the church in Colossae talks about this. Even though he addresses 'slaves', which Joseph was, it applies to us all:

> Slaves, obey your earthly masters in everything; and do it, not only when their eye is on you and to curry their favour, but with sincerity of heart and reverence for the Lord. Whatever you do, work at it with all your heart, as working for the Lord, not for human masters, since you know that you will receive an inheritance from the Lord as a reward.
> (Colossians 3:22–24).

Time for reconciliation

After Joseph had been in prison for some time, it seemed that God was going to rescue him through Pharaoh's cupbearer, who was being released from the jail. Sadly, this came to nothing and he was left languishing in prison (Genesis 40).

Later still, Pharaoh had a series of troubling dreams but no one could offer any explanation. Finally, the cupbearer remembered the dream interpreter in prison and Pharaoh summoned Joseph. He interpreted Pharaoh's dreams and predicted seven years of abundance followed by seven years of famine. He also gave Pharaoh a job description for someone discerning and wise who would be able to prepare the people for these periods. Unsurprisingly Joseph landed the job himself.

When the famine came, Egypt was well prepared, but the surrounding lands were not. People came from all around seeking food. In an incredible twist of fate, ten of Joseph's brothers ended up standing in front of him, the governor of Egypt. They hadn't brought Benjamin, his only full brother, as Jacob was too scared of losing him, so wouldn't allow him to travel. Joseph recognised the brothers instantly, but they had no idea it was him.

He accused the family of being spies and put them in prison, telling them they would be released if they brought Benjamin, the brother who had been left at home, to Egypt. Joseph also said that one brother had to stay behind as surety. Reuben's reaction to this was enlightening. He saw what was happening as comeuppance for the wrong they had done to Joseph. In a sense it really was a reckoning, as Joseph was testing them. He had changed over the years, but had they? Could there be reconciliation?

There is an important distinction between forgiveness and reconciliation. Principally, forgiving someone is about letting *ourselves* off the hook, rather than them. When we don't forgive, we stay locked into the pain of what happened. We remain stuck in a cycle of the past event holding on to us as we hold on to it, however subconsciously.

Imagine for a moment that you are walking along a riverbank on a sunny day. (It could be a rainy day, the point will be the same, but I assumed you'd prefer the warm weather!) You walk past a fisherman just as he goes to cast his line, and somehow the line catches you and the hook ends up in your cheek. It doesn't matter how much it hurts or whose fault it is; the priority is disconnecting yourself from the line and getting the hook out. Otherwise, as you carry on with your life, that hook and line will always be pulling you back. You're not doing it for the fisherman's sake, but for your own.

Forgiveness is the first step on the journey of our healing. It can be an ongoing process as more hurt and pain surfaces. It is like layers of an onion, or a parfait, as Donkey from *Shrek* would say. Forgiveness can open up the path to healing as we begin to engage more deeply with what we are forgiving the person for. It is not simply about what they did or didn't do, but the effect it had on us. How did it make us feel? What lie did it give root to?

Forgiveness does not mean that the person is let off the consequences of their actions. We can forgive someone and they may still need to face punishment or the cost of their actions. It also doesn't necessarily mean restoring or reconciling the relationship. Those are secondary to the action of forgiveness. For us to find true freedom, to remove the fish hook from our cheek, we need to forgive the other person whether they accept responsibility or not. But there can't be real reconciliation unless they accept what happened and change accordingly. Forgiveness is our work alone, whereas reconciliation is dependent on the actions of the person who caused the hurt. This is why Joseph tested his brothers' values and attitudes.

Changing character

Joseph sent the brothers away to fetch Benjamin, while keeping Simeon. Little did they know that he had hidden the money they paid for the grain in their sacks. Later, when they discovered money in one of their sacks, their instant assumption was that God was judging them. Their guilt for their actions against Joseph had clearly never left them. When they got home to Jacob, they discovered that all their money had been returned and they were frightened. Jacob's reaction to what had happened is fascinating. He was totally self-absorbed. He blamed them for losing Joseph and now Simeon. He saw everything as being against him (Genesis 42:36) and was unwilling to send Benjamin to Egypt. He'd rather lose Simeon than Benjamin. Reuben offered the lives of his own sons as a guarantee that they would bring Benjamin back, but Jacob was resolute. But, eventually the famine got so bad that they had no choice but to return for more grain. Jacob was still unwilling to let Benjamin go, but Judah persuaded him, offering his own life if anything were to happen.

They returned to Joseph with the original money, more money and gifts. Joseph said that the return of their money on the first occasion must have been down to their God, because he had received the money from them. As soon as he saw Benjamin, he was overcome and hurried off to weep. They then feasted together before he sent them home with their fresh grain. This time, though, Joseph again hid money in their bags and also slipped his own silver cup into Benjamin's bag.

Joseph sent his steward after them to accuse them of taking the cup. They were incredulous and said that if one of them had it, he should be put to death and the rest would become slaves. The steward said that if one of them had it, he would be a slave and the others would be free to go. He found the cup in Benjamin's sack. The brothers were distraught. They tore their clothes and returned to the city. They pleaded with Joseph and told him about Jacob. Judah beseeched Joseph to take him in Benjamin's place. The test was complete. The self-absorbed brothers who had once sold a brother into slavery would now give their lives for a brother. It was time for reconciliation. Joseph couldn't stand it any more and finally revealed his identity to his brothers.

Simeon, Reuben and Judah were all willing to sacrifice themselves for the sake of the wider family. This was in stark contrast to Jacob. If anything, Jacob seemed more caught up in his own self-obsessed grief and self-pity than before. He had risked the lives of all his sons for that of Benjamin.

I don't think everyone improves with age. As someone once said, we become 'better or bitter'. As some people age, their world shrinks and becomes more self-focused, with a sense that they are owed the time and investment of others. For others, their world stays outward-focused.

My childhood was full of older people. My mum was Chairperson and then President of Plymouth Age Concern. I vividly remember that our Christmas Days were centred around visiting an old people's home for drinks with the residents. When I was a curate, my favourite part of the week was Friday morning prayer with people who were four times my age. When we ran a church focused on reaching young people, my constant prayer was for grandparent-aged people to join the church. Older people are often the backbone of churches and not given the appreciation they deserve.

When we were in Birmingham, there was the most amazing couple in their eighties who offered pastoral support to the whole staff team. They were the safe place for everyone to go and offload and be prayed for. What constantly amazed me with them was that they were always talking about the new things they were learning about God. Their world was constantly expanding.

The wonderful thing with God is that he doesn't treat us as we deserve. Scripture is shot through with grace, and in spite of Jacob's attitude, he was welcomed back with open arms and abundant weeping (Genesis 46:29). God's generosity is more extravagant, even when it is undeserved.

As we get older and can't do what we used to do, rather than become resentful we should be looking to God to discover what we *can* do instead. I love the account of an old lady in a large church who was asked to help give out communion one day. For some reason, she'd never been asked to do it before and the church leader was surprised that she began to cry as she did it. They asked her afterwards why she had been crying. She said that a few years previously she had chatted to the youth worker about the fact that she was less and less able to help at church, but the one thing she could do was pray. She had then asked him whether she could pray for the young people. He had given her a photo of each young person and she had put them all over her house. Two photos were by the basin in her bathroom. Each night she prayed for those two young people as she cleaned her teeth. Another two were by the kettle and she prayed for them as she waited for it to boil. That morning, during communion, she had been looking into the eyes of these young people whom she had faithfully loved and prayed for several times a day for years but had never spoken to. She demonstrates a wonderful example of the blessing of old age and a heart that has matured in godliness.

A sad little tangent

Hidden in the middle of the story of Joseph is an account of one of his brothers that will never be made into a musical (Genesis 38). It is a shocking, shameful incident, which one might be tempted to skip over.

It is the only story that focuses on Judah. It tells of how he married a Canaanite woman, whose name we aren't even given. She gave birth to three sons: Er, Onan and Shelah. Judah found a wife for his first-born, Er – a woman called Tamar. Er was so bad that God killed him. There's no further explanation; just that he was 'wicked in the LORD's sight; so the LORD put him to death' (verse 7). We've covered a lot of bad behaviour that has apparently gone unpunished, yet Er was struck down for his. He must have been bad. His family wouldn't have known the cause of death. Death was so commonplace in those days, it was unlikely to have been seen as direct divine intervention.

Judah turned to son number two and told him it was his duty to produce a son with Tamar. Although this sounds unusual to us, it was standard practice in those days. An unmarried brother would take his brother's widow, and their first child was then seen as the child of the deceased brother. The first-born child would then carry on the name and line of this deceased brother.

Onan wasn't prepared to follow this protocol. We aren't told why. But we do know that he opted for a basic contraceptive method: coitus interruptus or withdrawal, or as the Bible puts it 'he spilled his semen' (verse 9). Over the years people have made much of this. Many have taken a strong line on it, including Jerome, Clement of Alexandria, Calvin and John Wesley. They focused on the wrongs of sexual activity being undertaken for reasons other than procreation. But, as is stated in the biblical account, the sin was not that he prevented procreation, but rather that he refused to honour his brother's name and line. It was also not an argument about whether the practice of producing an heir for your deceased brother was right or wrong, but rather about his attitude within the practice of the day. There was something significant about him dishonouring and shaming his sister-in-law in not doing the right thing by her and denying her a child. Like his brother, Onan was judged and he died. Judah started to realise something was not quite right. But instead of wondering about his children, he decided that Tamar was to blame for the death of his sons. We can so easily be blind when it comes to those we love or be blinded by the culture of our day.

Judah let Tamar stay at his house but held back his last son, Shelah, from marrying her for fear he would die too. Tamar wasn't destitute, but as a widow within her father-in-law's house she had no prospects and no future. Women had no rights in those days. They were regarded as the property of men. Tamar had to obey Judah and relied on him for food and shelter. She couldn't earn a living. She couldn't leave the house without his permission. Under the law she was supposed to marry his youngest son, so couldn't accept any other marriage proposals. She was beholden to a family who didn't want her and was destined to spend the rest of her days waiting for a marriage that Judah had no intention of allowing her.

A while later, Mrs Judah died. We never learn her name either. As he began to recover from his immediate grief, Judah went to Timnah for sheep shearing, as one did in those days. Tamar found out his plans and decided to take matters into her own hands. She changed out of her black widow's clothes, put on a veil and sat at the entrance to Enaim, on the way to Timnah. Judah, on seeing her, didn't recognise her and assumed she was a prostitute. It seems that Tamar knew this would happen. When he asked her for sex, she asked about payment. Apparently, Judah had gone out without his wallet, and Apple Pay was centuries away, so he couldn't pay up front. By way of deposit, she asked for the pledge of his seal, its cord and his staff. He agreed and they had sex.

Tamar got pregnant. She went back to wearing black and acted as if nothing had happened until she outgrew her clothes. In the meantime Judah returned to pay his debt to the prostitute, only to discover that no prostitutes operated in that area. It made no sense to him, but he decided to leave quietly rather than risk becoming a laughing stock. Three months later he was told that Tamar was guilty of prostitution, and pregnant. He demanded that she be burned to death. This was the harshest penalty possible, normally only reserved for daughters of priests who were guilty of prostitution.

She produced Judah's seal, cord and staff in her defence. At that moment Judah got it. The whole sorry story became clear to him. He declared that she was more righteous than he was since he wouldn't let her marry his son Shelah.

Is this just a moment in the family history that we should draw a veil over and pretend never happened? Couldn't we just remember Judah as better than most of his brothers in coming up with the idea of selling Joseph rather than killing him, and the one who gave his name to the Southern Kingdom? Because God appears to have simply turned a blind eye to this incident. There is nothing in the account to say that Judah did wrong in sleeping with a prostitute, let alone his daughter-in-law. His sons died for their sin, but his name lived on and eventually Jesus would come from his line. It is somewhat incredible that the story is included at all.

Yet God didn't want this story to be airbrushed out of the Bible. He didn't try to justify it. God does not condone violence or the mistreating of women, or indeed anyone. Repeatedly in Scripture he fights for victims and for those without a voice. In Tamar's story we see that God brought redemption by exposing the shameful secret. She was declared righteous. Furthermore, her story is raised again at the very start of the New Testament in the attestation of Jesus' lineage (Matthew 1:1–16). A pure lineage was vitally important to a good Jew. Yet in Jesus' family tree Matthew highlights the opposite. A lineage passes from father to son, down the males of the family. Yet Matthew shockingly draws attention to five women. Five women who undermined all Jewish ideas of a good family tree. One of them was Tamar. Jesus was descended from Perez, the illegitimate child of Tamar and her father-in-law Judah. However messed up our families or our past or our actions are, God is a God of restoration and redemption. It doesn't matter what dirty secrets you or your family have; they are not beyond God's love and power. What a relief!

Liz and I used to be involved with education in sex and relationships at some high schools. One of the most powerful things we ever did was to help with a session on marriage. Couples would come in and spend a morning sitting in front of two or three classes of young people in Years 9 and 10. Each class would see three different couples and they could ask them anything they liked about their relationship. The couple would only talk about what was asked and the students were totally in charge of the session. Nothing was off the table. As long as they behaved respectfully, they could ask literally anything.

As you would expect, one lad would invariably start the conversation by trying to be shocking, asking questions about favourite positions or locations for sex and so on. What tended to happen was the couple would respond, totally unfazed, and the lad would find it too awkward to ask anything else. After the obvious questions were exhausted, and the pupils had failed to embarrass the couple, it would often get more interesting. The pupils would ask about disciplining children, how they resolved arguments, how they knew they loved each other and so on.

Those sessions enabled young people to grapple with relationships over and above sex. It was probably the only time they would ever get to talk to adults about these things and gain insights from families outside their own.

The most powerful sessions always involved one particular couple. If I'm honest, outwardly they appeared boring and old. But as the questions flowed, it would transpire that their story was far from straightforward. She had grown up in a children's home. At eighteen, she was sent off with a suitcase and no support. She ended up living with a couple, and the man began to abuse her. Eventually she left and joined a church. In time she married, and all seemed to be going well, but something was eating away inside her. She would see girls with their dads and be consumed with a hunger for that kind of relationship. She ended up having an affair with a man old enough to be her father. Inevitably her husband found out, and she ended the affair and amazingly they managed to hold the marriage together.

As she shared her life story with different classes over the years, it was always incredibly emotional. There was such power in her being able to tell the young people that no matter what has happened or will happen in our lives, it doesn't need to dictate our future. Nothing can write us off as people. Tamar's life could so easily have been written off, but instead she is part of Jesus' family line.

Conclusion

When Jacob died, the brothers began to panic that Joseph might still be holding a grudge against them but had not acted on it for the sake of their father. Joseph famously responded, 'You intended to harm me, but God intended it for good to accomplish what is now being done, the saving of many lives' (Genesis 50:20). Joseph carried no bitterness or resentment for what his brothers did to him. Back when they were young, the brothers had wanted to ruin his life. This didn't justify what they did and it didn't let them off the hook. It was still wrong. Yet nothing is beyond God's redemption.

As we heard with Abraham, Romans 8:28 says: 'And we know that in all things God works for the good of those who love him, who have been called according to his purpose.' This is often used to argue for God's sovereign purposes behind some terrible occurrence, as if it's OK for this to happen because God is working for good behind it. I believe it is far fairer to God's character and to Scripture to say that whatever the cause of an event, God can work out some good purpose.

If God's sovereignty is behind all that happens on earth, the logical conclusion is that he is the instigator of evil. But this can't be true. James 1:13 says, 'God cannot be tempted by evil, nor does he tempt anyone.' Rather God gives us free will. Things will happen that God doesn't actively choose or even want to happen. But God's grace means that he can redeem our deepest mistakes and sins and bring good out of them.

Joseph began life as an arrogant, spoiled and entitled young man. He ruined his relationship with his brothers so badly that he was nearly killed. This began a series of twists and turns that left him imprisoned with seemingly no way out. Throughout Joseph's life, God not only changed his character but rescued the people of Israel and Egypt from starvation, famine and death. If God can do that through Joseph, what about us? Let's not write ourselves off.

Part 2

THE PRINCE OF EGYPT

4

The prince of Egypt

Setting the scene

In spite of all Joseph did to rescue the Egyptians from famine and disaster, their gratitude quickly faded. No sooner had Joseph's generation died out than the Egyptians forgot his part in their history (Exodus 1). A new pharaoh came to power and all he could see was an increasing immigrant population and the potential threat they presented. Sadly it seems that immigration and prejudice has been a problem throughout history. Fear can so quickly lead to irrational responses and actions. Through fear, Pharaoh forced the Israelites into slavery, yet the more they were oppressed the more they multiplied.

Heroines of faith

Pharaoh was so desperate to neutralise the perceived threat that he turned to genocide. He told the Hebrew midwives to kill all Israelite boys at birth.[1] But in an unexpected twist, the midwives disobeyed him. He reacted by ordering all Israelite baby boys to be thrown into the Nile. He really wasn't keen on immigrants!

As all of this was happening, one couple had a beautiful baby boy who was too fine to kill (Exodus 2). One would suspect all parents feel that their new baby boy is too fine to kill but, as the New Testament reports, there was something about this baby that made

---

1   I tend to use the terms 'Israelite' and 'Hebrew' interchangeably, since they refer to the same people. Strictly speaking in the Old Testament God's people are initially known as the Hebrews and later called the Israelites, but there's some mixed use. The New Testament refers to them by both names.

his parents realise he was 'no ordinary child' (Acts 7:20; Hebrews 11:23). They kept him hidden for three whole months before realising they couldn't conceal a crying baby for much longer. His mum amazingly made a little floating Moses basket for him (which is a coincidence, what with that being his name[2]), placed him in it and pushed it out into the Nile. In one sense this woman was obeying Pharaoh, as she was throwing him into the Nile as ordered, albeit very carefully. His big sister Miriam watched from a distance to see what would become of the baby.

It just so happened that at this moment Pharaoh's daughter came to bathe in the river and discovered the basket floating in the reeds. She had compassion on the child, realising that he was a Hebrew baby, and therefore doomed to be killed. Just as she was wondering what to do, Miriam bravely approached and offered to bring a Hebrew woman to nurse the baby for her. The princess readily agreed. Miriam fetched her mum.

Moses was not only saved from death in the Nile, he was saved *by* the Nile. He was brought up in the palace of the man who had ordered his death, by that man's very own daughter. Sounds awkward! His daughter was incredibly brave to defy her father, the most powerful man in Egypt. Moses received an education in the most privileged place possible. Not only that, in his early years Pharaoh paid Moses' mum to raise him, giving her the opportunity to teach him about his culture and about God (Exodus 1:9–10). God really does know how to take the worst evil and completely turn it on its head.

All the heroes of this account are women: the midwives, Moses' mum, his sister Miriam and the princess. Pharaoh is not even given a name, much to the distress of many theologians over the ages trying to date this story. Yet the midwives, who were more concerned for God's law than with Pharaoh's edicts, are named:

---

2 Sorry – terrible dad joke! Couldn't resist!

Shiphrah and Puah. In saving the lives of the Hebrew babies they risked their own and ultimately saved a nation. Moses' mum was willing to put her own life on the line by hiding her baby, as was Miriam when she bravely approached Pharaoh's daughter. Pharaoh's daughter knew she had found a Hebrew baby, yet she took him home and raised him in direct contravention of her dad's instructions. All five women were in a place of powerlessness in their society. All five women were subject to the rule of men. All five women managed to subvert Pharaoh's evil plan and play a part in God's rescue.

I recently heard Maryam Rostampour and Marziyeh Amirizadeh speaking about their experiences in Iran.[3] Both born into Muslim families, they met in 2005 while studying in Turkey, having both separately converted to Christianity six years earlier. Although it's illegal to share the Christian faith in Iran, they passionately believed that people needed to discover Jesus. So, upon returning, they decided to share their faith by systematically distributing Farsi New Testaments throughout Tehran. They placed them in mailboxes, restaurants and even the back of taxis, ultimately distributing 20,000 copies across the city. The authorities thought a covert Christian organisation was operating in the city. Little did they know that it was just two women in their twenties. At the same time, Maryam and Marziyeh established two house churches in their apartment – one for young people and another for prostitutes.

In 2009, they were arrested for promoting Christianity, which is punishable by death. They were imprisoned for 259 days in Tehran's notorious Evin prison. Their experiences sound horrendous, but despite enduring severe mistreatment, they saw it as an opportunity to share their faith within the very prison that was meant to silence them. Like the midwives, it's staggering what two women can do

---

3   Their book *Captive in Iran* (Illinois: Tyndale House, 2013) is well worth a read.

when they trust God more than they fear an authority trying to suppress faith.

Failing in leadership

Moses was destined for big things. He was brought up as a prince, but he knew where he came from. As an adult, he went back to visit his own people at work (Exodus 2:11).[4] He watched the Israelites' back-breaking labour making bricks for the Egyptians. He saw one of them being beaten by an Egyptian slave master. He intervened, and ended up killing the slave master. He hid the body, thinking no one had seen him. The next day he returned and this time witnessed two Hebrews fighting. Again, he couldn't help but intervene. They asked if he was going to kill them too, as he had the man from the previous day. He realised he had been found out; that his crime hadn't gone unnoticed. News of the attack even made it back to Pharaoh himself. Pharaoh set out to kill Moses for a second time, so Moses fled for his life to Midian.

Moses had been trained in leadership from an early age. At the same time he had a heart for injustice and a desire to see his people set free. He was ready to live as a Hebrew instead of an Egyptian prince (Hebrews 11:24). As we hear in Acts 7:25, when he defended the Hebrew slave he expected the people to realise God would use him to rescue them. Imagine his horror then when instead it was thrown back in his face the next time he tried to help his people. These men asked a profound question: 'Who made you ruler and

---

4 Interestingly, the original account in Exodus does not tell us how old Moses was at this point. But by some cunning maths (our son would be proud!) we can make an estimate. Moses died aged 120 (Deuteronomy 34:7). Before this he spent forty years wandering in the wilderness with the people of Israel and forty years in the land of Midian. We don't actually know how long Moses took arguing with Pharaoh, but Moses was probably around forty when this incident took place. It is interesting that what I think of as an age definitely beyond youth the Bible merely describes as grown up. It makes sense though. I felt so grown up in my twenties, yet beyond my forties I'm much more aware of how young that was!

judge over us?' (Exodus 2:14). That must have devastated him. In his mind, at least in some way, God had called him to lead them, but the men didn't recognise this. Moses felt that he had completely failed, so he gave up and ran away.

In today's instant society it's so easy to give up and run away from challenges and even failures. If we make a mistake, it can be easier to decide we're a failure and run away rather than face up to it. Maybe we face relationship challenges, we've let someone we love down, and rather than work to rebuild the trust, it seems easier to close part of ourselves off and walk away. But failure is not fatal. In fact, it can be the start of great change and growth. A wise vicar from my past used to say that you should never leave a job simply to escape from a tough situation. We need to try to work things through and then leave well. This applies to more than just a work context.

We encounter challenge and failure in every area of our lives, in work situations, in churches, in families and in relationships. In them all we need to try to find some sense of resolution and then think about leaving. If we simply run away from situations that seem too hard, we take the issues with us. Time and again people leave a relationship thinking the problem is with the other person and don't notice that the pattern continues in the next relationship.

I have met many people who have felt called into some form of ministry, but something has gone wrong and they have been left crushed by the experience. Like Moses many people have leadership gifts, but in their early attempts to lead they end up being rejected. Sometimes this causes them to force their leadership on to others or vow never to try to lead again. When I was fifteen, I used to be involved with all sorts of evangelism. I tried sharing my faith with my friends and even went door to door by myself in a somewhat dubious block of flats in Plymouth. I was mildly successful at this and various members of my year from school started coming to our church youth group. But then, for a multitude of reasons, not only did those enquiring about faith turn away, but they also took lots of the committed youth with them. This and some other failed attempts at evangelism meant I felt useless as an evangelist and ran away from sharing my faith. I'd encourage and lead others in evangelism but avoid doing it myself. It wasn't until we started thinking about planting a church to reach unchurched youth, more than fifteen years later, that I had to face this past hurt and failure. I recognised that I turned away from an area of ministry God had called me to. Many of us have had our fingers burned when we've bravely stepped out. Sometimes we then assume that we got it wrong and never explore that godly yearning again. When we run away from what God has made us to be and do, we and the world miss out.

God had destined Moses to be the one who led his people into freedom. But here, Moses wasn't going about it in God's way. He took things upon himself, before the time was right. Perhaps God had instilled a sense of justice in him, but by expressing it in his own way, without appropriate wisdom, Moses ended up ultimately committing a murder. This led to forty years of hiding before God could bring him out to fulfil his calling. We need to trust God and do things in his way, at his speed. We need boundaries. Jesus says that his yoke is easy and his burden is light (Matthew 11:30), yet I meet with so many church leaders who are bent over with the weight of all they are doing. Some of this is down to the unreasonable expectations and demands of leadership structures, but it can also be down to people carrying things they shouldn't be. Someone once described it to me as 'unauthorised compassion'. Leaders are called to care for people and have compassion for them, but that doesn't mean they need to take on everyone's needs. If they do, they quickly become overwhelmed and are consequently less able to care for those they are meant to be supporting.

It also means they get in the way of the right people being able to use their gifts. I used to know a teenage girl who clearly had a real pastoral heart and gifting. Sadly, because of her need to be needed and her insecurities, she seemed constantly to smother people. Instead of offering pastoral support she became more of a pastoral problem. God calls us and equips us, but he doesn't call us to do everything. He doesn't ask us to go beyond our call and our character. We also need to be working from his strength and motivation.

Running away from what's meant to be

Moses fled to Midian and we're told that when he arrived he sat down to rest by a well. He must have felt so low. While he sat there, caught up in his own dejection, seven daughters of a Midianite priest came to water their flocks. As he watched, some shepherds began to harass them and stop them getting to the water. Moses couldn't help himself. He stood up for them, intervening and rescuing them. He had run away, but he couldn't escape himself or what God had made him to be.

Cutting to the chase and skipping over the courtship and engagement, he married one of the shepherd girls. They loved each other very much and had a baby. They called him Gershom. As we've come to expect, his name has a meaning. From the Hebrew, it means 'to drive, cast out', recalling that Moses was driven out of Egypt in fear for his life. But it is also a play on the sound of the words that combine to form his name, as the narrator explains: 'I have become a foreigner in a foreign land' (Exodus 2:22). Moses had found love and started a family, but it wasn't where he belonged.

When we're disappointed with God or feel we've failed, it can be easier to run away from who we really are. It's easy to have dreams of changing the world when we're young, but then life bulldozes through those dreams. Over time we accumulate a busy job, a mortgage and children. Don't get me wrong. I'm not saying that all our youthful dreams can become a reality, or even that they are all from God. In my work with young people, I've been surprised by the number I've talked to whose aspiration is simply to be famous. In an age of TV talent shows it has become easy for people to believe that they can have fame, just for the sake of it, without developing any real talent.

God can instil a passion in us that we shouldn't give up on. At fifty, I look around and see many of my contemporaries who are halfway through their working life in a job they can barely tolerate. But they are now trapped by financial and family constraints. Life has crowded in and crowded out their youthful dreams. They have settled.

Called by God

Objection 1: Who am I?

One day, Moses was out looking after his father-in-law's flocks in Mount Horeb, which one translation of the Bible descriptively calls 'the backside of the desert'.[5] Forty or so years had passed since Moses left Egypt, so he was now around eighty. His childhood must have become a distant memory, the stuff of bedtime stories for his kids. These days, he was a simple shepherd, working for his in-laws in the back of beyond.

This particular day, he noticed a bush on fire, which was not an uncommon occurrence in the desert. Moses was intrigued. Perhaps anything was a welcome distraction from the monotony of his work. But Moses' attention was caught as he realised the bush was not being burnt up by the fire. As soon as he approached, God spoke to him from the bush. He spoke of rescuing his people from Egypt. You can imagine Moses nodding along at this point, his excitement

---

5 This is at the beginning of Exodus 3 in the King James Version. Often the language of the King James Version is quite formal and hard to understand easily, but this phrase captures the scene perfectly!

growing. He had tried to act against the injustices inflicted on the people of God, but had failed ignominiously. He now lived in exile for his actions. Yet he was hearing that God himself would intervene. Moses must have felt over the moon ... right up until the moment when God told him that he, Moses, would be the means of liberating them.

Moses was incredulous and probably more than a little terrified. Yahweh (God) partnering with humanity was unheard of. Abraham was called by God, but there was no sense that he was being given a mission. As far as Moses was concerned, God asking him to help set his people free was ridiculous. He knew he had already tried and failed. He thought he had nothing much to offer to God. However, with Moses, God was starting a whole new phase in his relationship with his people. God was still God – his plan would come to fruition – but from this point onwards he would partner with humanity. And in this case, the freeing of his people from slavery in Egypt would happen specifically with Moses.

Moses' first reply to this staggering commission was, 'Who am I?' (Exodus 3:11). God could so easily have answered, 'What do you mean, "Who am I?"? Moses, I have been planning this since before you were born. Look at your CV! You are the only Hebrew man of your age. You were plucked from death to be raised as a prince. Your whole childhood was preparing you for this moment. You are an Egyptian prince and a Hebrew leader. You are the only person for the job. You can talk with Pharaoh because you grew up with him in his palace. My preparation for this was ingenious. This is what you were born to! Oh, Moses!' Instead, God simply said, 'I will be with you.' He didn't answer the question at all and yet he answered it completely. Who Moses was didn't matter at all. What mattered was who God was and that God was with him.

It's all too easy for the success or failure of a team to rest on its leaders. There are any number of personality-type profiling methods to help discern how a person thinks and acts, and how these traits influence their leadership. These are all valuable tools in helping us understand ourselves and be more effective. However, Christian faith and leadership are about the God who is with us far more than they are about us. God's answer underlines that he, God, is the subject, not Moses. In his opening address to Moses he said, '*I* have indeed seen … *I* have heard … *I* am concerned … *I* have come down to rescue … *I* have seen … *I* am sending you …' (Exodus 3:7–10, my italics).

Recently I heard Stephen Foster, the leader of St Aldate's Church in Oxford, talking about an early experience of being called. Years ago he was asked to help with the youth group. He responded, 'It's not a good time for me. I'm busy with work. Family life is pressured …' The youth leader replied, 'But it's a really good time for the youth.' Stephen tried again, saying, 'I wouldn't be very good at it. Surely there are better people than me?' The youth leader responded, 'Undoubtedly there are people who would be better at this than you. But I'm asking you.' The same two thoughts probably occur to most people when they are called by God. We look at ourselves, and that is not the point of calling. It is not about us. It is about the one who is calling us.

Moses was not alone in needing the reassurance 'I am with you'. Joshua, Moses' successor, was promised, 'As I was with Moses, so I will be with you' (Joshua 1:5). It's interesting to note that this declaration from God was much more reassuring than one Joshua received later, when the Israelites promised, 'Just as we fully obeyed Moses, so we will obey you' (Joshua 1:17). Given how bad they were at following Moses, there couldn't have been a less reassuring assertion.

Centuries later, when Jeremiah objected to God's call because he was 'too young' and didn't 'know how to speak', God promised to be with him too (Jeremiah 1:4–8). One of the last things Jesus said to his disciples was that he would be with them: 'I will not leave you as orphans; I will come to you' (John 14:18). When we are called into leadership, it's never about our abilities. It is always about God's presence with us. On the whole, I find this to be a great relief!

Sometimes, though, being told that God is with us just doesn't help. Many of us have experienced trauma or disappointment while God was supposedly with us. We can be left asking, 'So what if God is with me? It hasn't made any difference. God didn't help me.' We are not alone in feeling this. We see people in the Bible questioning God constantly. For example, when an angel said to Gideon, 'The LORD is with you, mighty warrior.' Gideon basically responded, 'Well, that's a fat lot of good!' (Judges 6:11–16). Gideon's words were honest and raw.

It's important in our faith not to bury or ignore our pain, but to bring it to God. If we say with our mouths that we trust God, but deep within we feel something different, our faith won't survive. What we see in Gideon's example is that although God didn't directly answer his complaint, something shifted in Gideon after he began to grapple with the call. As God carried on explaining this call, Gideon asked, 'How can I save Israel?' God replied, 'I will be with you.' Even then Gideon famously laid out fleeces as a test for God before he was convinced. People so often talk about laying a fleece before God, but I wonder if they are taking the wrong application from the passage. The take-home message is that honesty is important and we should allow God to meet us in our doubts.

Objection 2: Who are you?

Next, Moses asked who God was (Exodus 3:13). At eighty, Moses seems to have become the opposite of his younger self. Maybe the forty years since he ran away hadn't been wasted. He no longer believed that he was God's gift who could single-handedly save his people. As a young man he was desperate to lead. But when he was finally called, the objections kept flowing. How could he tell the Israelites that God had sent him when he didn't know God's name?

Moses already knew that he was in the presence of God, so by asking who God was, he was probably asking for something more than a name. Before Moses embarked on a mission that would be dangerous for himself and the Israelites, he wanted to know more about God.

There were many occasions when people asked Jesus questions, not because they wanted to know the answer, but because they wanted catch him out. For example, there was the expert in the law who asked Jesus what he had to do to inherit eternal life. The Bible says the question was asked as a test, but whatever the man's motives, Jesus used the question as an opportunity to teach one of his most famous parables, the Good Samaritan (Luke 10:25–37). Similarly, whatever Moses' motivation was, God used the question to reveal something that carried eternal significance.

As we have already seen, biblical names are highly significant. They reveal the character and story of the bearer. God's response is enigmatic. Many translations record his answer as 'I AM WHO I AM'. But the translation is a little trickier than that! In fact, many theologians have puzzled over it. In the original Hebrew there is a sense that God is, always has been and will be for ever. There is an eternal nature to the statement. Ultimately, God is beyond names and descriptions. He always has been and always will be. *He is.* This is a title Jesus would take upon himself. John recorded Jesus frequently using an 'I am' refrain as part of his descriptions of himself.

God is not afraid of our questions or put off by our mixed motives. I loved it when our children were questioning everything around them – 'But *why*, Daddy?!' It was delightful (if a little exhausting) – much more endearing than the arrogant teenage years when children know everything.

Often people feel they need to filter their prayers or that God will be irritated by their repeated questioning. The opposite is true. God loves it when we wrestle with our understanding.

Questions are a key part of a parent/child relationship. God is far more comfortable with a constant barrage of 'But why?!' than most parents are!

Objection 3: What if they don't believe me?

God went on to describe exactly what would happen when Moses began to lead, even describing the miracles that would accompany the words. He made sure to say that the elders of Israel would listen to him (Exodus 3:18). Moses listened to God's clear explanation of what to expect and instantly retorted, 'What if they do not believe me or listen to me?' (Exodus 4:1). God then gave Moses three signs, with a three-fold purpose: to convince first Moses, then the people and finally Pharaoh that God was able to save his people. All three signs struck at the power of Pharaoh and revealed God as the ultimate giver of life and ruler of all.

One of the signs involved Moses throwing the shepherd's staff in his hand on the ground, where it instantly became a snake. As I am 'mildly' scared of snakes, this would have totally convinced me! But more than simply being terrifyingly awesome, there was another layer of meaning to the sign. The snake symbolised the power of Pharaoh and was worshipped as a god in Egypt. God demonstrated his ultimate power by subduing the snake completely.

The staff becoming a snake made a hugely significant statement that God alone is God. But it also made a more personal point: God transformed the shepherd's staff in Moses' hand into something beyond comprehension, while calling him to be a shepherd to God's people. In the New Testament, some of the disciples were told to lay down their fishing nets as they were called to become fishers of men. If we take what we have and throw it down before God, he can transform it. When we offer our paltry gifts to God, he imbues them with incomparable value and power.

Jesus demonstrated something similar, exponentially multiplying the loaves and fishes of a small boy to feed a crowd of 5,000.

Whatever we have in our hands – our gifts, passions and resources – we are called to lay it before God for him to use.

Objection 4: I'm a rubbish speaker

The fourth excuse Moses produced was that he wasn't articulate enough. He said he was 'slow of speech and tongue' (Exodus 4:10). This really does feel like an excuse, especially as he was described by Stephen in Acts 7:22 as being 'powerful in speech'. Also, although Aaron would become his spokesman on numerous occasions, Moses did speak for himself. God didn't dismiss this objection or tell him to get over it. Instead, he pointed out that he, God, was responsible for speech in the first place and could easily help him speak. Again, by focusing on himself rather than God, Moses missed the fact that God would be with him.

He wasn't alone in his fear of public speaking. Many people with crippling speech impediments have had incredibly successful careers relying on their voices, like Emily Blunt, Bruce Willis and Nicole Kidman. Others managed to work with their stammers, like former President of the US Joe Biden and Winston Churchill. For *Mr Bean* actor Rowan Atkinson, it was part of what created his unique style. For singers such as Ed Sheeran, it led them to the microphone. What the world sees as a barrier doesn't have to stop you. And that's even before we consider God's involvement. Where God calls, it's OK to trust him, even if it seems unlikely. As Mary said when presented with the concept of the virgin birth, 'With God nothing shall be impossible' (Luke 1:37, KJV).

Send someone else!

Finally, Moses cut to the chase and said, 'Pardon your servant, Lord. Please send someone else' (Exodus 4:13). He just didn't want to do it. At this point, the Bible says that God got angry, but even so dealt with him gently. God said he would send his brother Aaron with him, as he could speak well. Moses could simply tell Aaron what to say and he would do the talking for him.

It's interesting what filters we bring when we read the Bible. What are we drawn to in this bit of the tale? Is it that God was angry or that he took Moses' objections seriously and provided a solution? His actions were not related to anger but stemmed from compassion. God can be angry and even disappointed at our sin, yet still act out of love towards us.

Even before Moses' protestations, God had it in hand. Before Moses began his catalogue of objections, God had already arranged for Aaron to be on his way to meet him. God knows our struggles and anxieties before we know them ourselves. It's so easy to call God 'Lord' and yet not believe it. We recognise him as Lord and then live as if he's not by trying to take control ourselves. But real faith involves obedience. As it says in the book of Hebrews, 'faith is confidence in what we hope for and assurance about what we do not see' (Hebrews 11:1). When the angel called the shepherds to visit the baby Jesus, the confirmation that they had done the right thing would be finding him wrapped in swaddling clothes, lying in a manger. By that time, they would have already left their sheep and taken all the risk.

Things get worse

Moses set off for Egypt to confront Pharaoh and ask him to let God's people, the Israelites, go. Before he got going, God reassured him that the people who wanted to kill him had died. But he also gently forewarned Moses that things wouldn't go well. God revealed that Pharaoh's heart would harden and that he wouldn't back down until his first-born son died.

Even with God's warning, it must have been hard for Moses to persevere in the face of Pharaoh's unwillingness to acquiesce. Little did Moses know that facing the imposing and immoveable figure of Pharaoh, viewed by the Egyptians as a deity himself, was nothing in comparison with the challenge the people of Israel would present!

Moses and Aaron's first meeting with the Israelites went well. They believed what Moses shared and the leaders ended up bowing down and worshipping God. So Moses went to Pharaoh and requested that he let the Israelites go and worship their God for three days in the desert. Pharaoh replied that not only could they not go, but the Israelite slaves would now have to find their own straw to produce just as many bricks, drastically increasing their workload.

The Israelites couldn't understand what on earth was going on. Confounded, they complained and were told that the new regime was punishment for asking for a mini-break to worship their God. The leaders instantly turned on Moses and accused him of putting their very lives in jeopardy. They claimed that they never asked for his intervention and he had only made matters worse.

We can hardly blame the Israelites for their reaction. This was a tough moment for them and Moses. They were desperate for their slavery to end, but instead of freedom, Pharaoh's oppression increased. Brick-making was back-breaking work, but they'd got used to it. They didn't like the pain, but at least it was familiar.

Are you willing to go through the fear and pain of healing? For example, you may hate being lonely, but at least it's a familiar emptiness and feels safer than letting others get too close, which risks rejection. Or you might want to be free from the effects of a past trauma, but finding that freedom would involve engaging with what happened, which would be painful and scary. That process, certainly initially, can be way more painful than living with things as they currently are. It takes courage to allow God to set you free. For the Israelites it would be a painful journey to freedom.

Why have you brought trouble?

Moses was understandably gutted and went straight back to God (Exodus 5:22). He blamed God for bringing trouble on the people. He blamed Pharaoh for bringing trouble on the people. He didn't once blame himself. However, Moses had been disobedient. God very clearly told him to go and meet Pharaoh with the leaders of the Israelites (Exodus 3:18). Yet he and Aaron went alone (Exodus 5:1). However, when he turned back to God, God didn't tell him off for his disobedience. God didn't roll his eyes and say, 'It's all your fault. What did you expect? Did you really think you could take on the most powerful person in the world in your own strength?' No. Instead, God reassured him. He reminded Moses of the plan and of all the incredible things he had done and was still to do. The focus was returned well and truly on God.

Moses was still worried that he wasn't able to speak convincingly enough to persuade anyone, but this time he did as God said. This time there was no running away or self-pity as in his youth. He trusted God.

When toddlers have a tantrum, they scream and lash out at their parents. Often the parents just take them in their arms and hold them safe until they calm down. It seems that this was what was happening here. Moses was railing at God, even though he had been warned how things would go. God didn't point out Moses' failings. He simply listened and then reiterated his reassurance.

I remember a speaker once talking about a time of immense struggle in his life. He became so desperate that he took a day out to pray on the moors. His prayer turned into a deluge of anger pointed at God. He ranted, raved and swore at God for what felt like hours. Eventually he got to the end of his tirade, and then had a sense of God responding with, 'Is that everything?' This unleashed a further outpouring of pain and tears, at the end of which he had a sense of God saying, 'Are you done?' Well, he wasn't done, and began a further outburst. He said that by the end of this torrent he was shattered, but realised that he had the most incredible sense of God's presence and peace. God didn't defend himself or point out the man's failings; he simply let him give full vent to what he was feeling, and then brought his reassurance to the depths of his being.

Leadership crisis

The tale of Israel's eventual escape from Egypt is amazing and the stuff of movies.[6] But we are going to jump ahead to see something more of Moses' leadership through the trials and tribulations of the desert.

Moses' leadership would be continually tested. At the outset, the Israelites found themselves hemmed in against the Red Sea, with the Egyptian army chasing them and closing in. The people instantly became melodramatic, declaring that Moses had only brought them into the desert to die. They said that they'd be better turning themselves over to the Egyptians. Only hours earlier they'd seen God's miraculous intervention, with the Egyptian people who'd enslaved them pouring silver, gold and clothing upon them (Exodus 12:35–36). How quickly they lost the plot. Moses said confidently to the people that they needed to trust, and God would deliver them. Intriguingly, the Bible reveals that while he said this confidently, internally he was screaming out to God for rescue. God responded to him, saying, 'Why are you crying out to me?' (Exodus 14:15).

Being a leader is tough. At this moment, Moses needed to reassure the people and keep his own fear and panic from them. But this didn't mean he had to bury what he was feeling. Instead, he poured it out to God. As leaders we are called to be real with those we lead, while at the same time setting an example. We need

---

6 Literally! You can pick your genre, from the animated *The Prince of Egypt* to *Exodus: Gods and Kings* to the classic 1950s *The Ten Commandments*.

to inspire confidence rather than widespread panic, while also showing integrity.

Simon P. Walker, in his book *The Undefended Leader*,[7] talks about a leader's front stage and back stage. Our private and public lives must reflect each other; they need to fit together. Too many leaders put up a front in ministry, showing themselves to be full of faith and genuine discipleship, when in private it's a totally different story. Eventually they can't keep up the pretence and it all comes crashing down. We need honesty. This doesn't mean, however, that it is helpful for us to be ruthlessly vulnerable with everyone; we need appropriate boundaries. Those we lead do not need to know our every weakness, foible and doubt.

We need different people and places where we can share at a deeper level. If we are married, honesty with our spouse is essential, but it may not always be helpful to share our every doubt and struggle with them. There should be people in our church we can be honest with, but again there will be some things it isn't helpful to share. In addition, it might be good to be part of a prayer triplet or peer cell that carries a commitment to accountability and support. For many, a spiritual director and/or mentor can provide a safe space for brutal honesty without having to worry about how what we share will impact the other person. I can be totally straight with my mentor about the doubts and temptations I am struggling with. We are friends, but in my mentoring sessions it is not a reciprocal relationship; it is totally focused on me, my faith journey and my leadership. I can safely share about anything without filters.

Then, of course, there is God. As we see with Moses, we can internally scream and be relentlessly honest with him, while smiling on the outside and reassuring people it's all OK!

---

7   Simon P. Walker, *The Undefended Leader* (Manchester: Piquant Editions, 2010).

God's provision

As soon as the Israelites crossed the sea, they worshipped God. But almost as soon as the final chorus ended, the complaining began. First, there wasn't water, so the people grumbled and Moses passed their complaints on to God, who miraculously made a bitter pool drinkable. But as they journeyed on, they turned a corner (if deserts have corners) and there was a beautiful oasis not only with water, but with twelve springs of water (Exodus 15:27).

Next, there wasn't food. This elicited complaints that they had been brought out to the desert to starve. They fondly remembered that in Egypt they'd had massive pots of meat and as much food as they could eat. This sounds more like an all-inclusive holiday than the slavery they had just left! How quickly our memories are warped. But again, God provided. This time it was a food called manna. God gave some very clear instructions around this food. He promised that there would be enough for everyone delivered fresh each morning, so they didn't need to – in fact, they mustn't – hoard it overnight. In addition, there wouldn't be any on the Sabbath, so the day before, they could collect double and it wouldn't go off. The people disregarded the instructions and many took extra on week days to keep overnight, which resulted in piles of rotting manna. They also went out on the Sabbath to collect food, which was just a waste of time.

The Israelites' journeys around the wilderness continued in the same vein. The people moaned, blaming and doubting God via Moses. Moses went to God, and he provided. It is amazing how quick they were to complain and how impatient they were for an answer. Time and again God was immensely gracious with them. He provided water, even though he knew that if they would just wait a little longer, they would stumble on an oasis. God could so easily have commanded them to trust or have more faith, yet instead he generously provided.

Human nature seems to assume that God will test us rather than recognise that God is abundantly generous to us. In contrast to God's patience, we are impatient. We want more and want to be in control. When he gives clear instructions, as with the manna, we ignore what we are told to do and try to take control. We have a tendency to push against the boundaries God gives us.

Time to delegate

Where the people were quick to disregard God's instructions, Moses learned to be sensitive to them. Over and over, he saw God's provision first-hand. His faith grew even as the people's continued to waver. Unsurprisingly, therefore, he began to take too much upon himself. He held leadership too tightly. In the end it was his father-in-law, Jethro, who challenged him when he came on a family visit (Exodus 18).

Jethro was a Midianite priest, who was likely to have been a follower of different gods rather than God himself. At the time, gods were seen as geographically bound – something the people were beginning to discover wasn't the case, as God remained with them when they moved from place to place. When Jethro heard all that God had done, whether he followed him before or not he declared that the God of the Israelites was greater than all other gods. He brought sacrifices to God. But despite seeing that God was good, when he observed that Moses had to deal with all the people's problems (big and small), he recognised that the set-up was not good.

Jethro showed immense wisdom and encouraged his son-in-law to delegate. Moses' intentions were good; he was all about helping the people seek God's will. Yet, as Jethro showed him, he could train up others to assist him. Jethro talked about carefully choosing the right people. He gave wise advice, but also recognised that wisdom alone wasn't enough. He concluded, 'If you do this and

God so commands, you will be able to stand the strain, and all these people will go home satisfied' (Exodus 18:23).

Jethro, who probably wasn't even a 'proper' believer, grasped a key concept: only a 'God idea' is helpful, rather than just a 'good idea'. Or to put it another way, 'Unless the LORD builds the house, its builders labour in vain' (Psalm 127:1). We must always seek God's will rather than just make a plan and ask God to bless it.

Jethro highlighted several other key leadership issues. He saw that we can burn out doing stuff God did not intend for us to do. He also saw that we can delegate aspects of ministry, yet still hold on to leadership too tightly. This was demonstrated when Moses sent Joshua to lead a battle against the Amalekites while he prayed on an overlooking hillside (Exodus 17:8ff.), yet he was still doing too much. This not only wore him out but also blocked others from using their gifts and growing in leadership. Healthy shared leadership is important both for those who lead and for those who are led.

Several years ago, I took my only ever sabbatical. It was the first time, other than for holidays, that my wife and I had been away from the church we'd led since we started it. We had to delegate like never before. It soon became clear quite how much I'd held the church back over the years by doing too much myself. Sometimes it had simply been through not wanting to add to people's already busy lives. I thought I was protecting them. I thought that I would rather take the slack myself than impose on them. But by releasing others more, we saw both them and the church flourish.

One of our sons stepped up in a Jethro moment last summer. He was helping at a big Christian event and was asked by the event leader for his reflections. He shared that the event leader was fantastic at recognising the gifts of others, but could delegate more, which in turn would allow the leader, the team and the event to flourish.

To Moses' credit, he not only listened to his father-in-law, but also did exactly what he suggested. I love good advice. I love hearing other people's wisdom. But I don't always find it easy to implement. Change can feel like an admission of failure, or like acknowledging that what we have been doing is wrong. That's hard to admit. But it isn't necessarily that what we've been doing is wrong; it might simply be that things have changed and it's time to adapt.

One of the high points of our ministry during our time leading Unlimited Church was running a night café. This café was open from midnight to three in the morning on a Friday or Saturday night for young people in need of sanctuary or support on a night out. Initially we opened monthly, but I longed to have enough team members to run it fortnightly and eventually weekly so that we would be a permanent, reliable night-time presence in the city centre. We had more exciting God encounters at the night café than at any other events we ran. In time we did manage to run it fortnightly. Then even more people joined the team. It became increasingly known about in the city, with the city council, police and university commending us for it.

Just as we were enjoying our success, and maybe feeling a little proud of our reputation, we began to notice that we were getting fewer visitors. The numbers dwindled to single figures, until one night absolutely no one came to the café, despite the city centre being as busy as ever. Interestingly this café came at the end of a week of prayer in which as a church family we were seeking God's wisdom for our outreach. The answer seemed clear, so with heavy hearts we decided to stop the night café. It wasn't an easy decision, nor one that we took lightly. The night café felt like the jewel in our crown. It was the edgy, exciting activity that seemed exactly what a church focused on unchurched youth should be all about. Closing it seemed like a backward step in our relationships with the community. We were worried about what people would think.

At about the same time, without connecting the two, we started a drop-in for younger youth. It was the kind of thing churches all over the country do. It wasn't pioneering or particularly edgy, but it was what God seemed to want us to do. We'd had it in mind for years, but it was only when the night café closed that we had enough volunteers to make it possible. Was the night café a mistake? Definitely not, but the time had come for change.

Having to make hard decisions doesn't necessarily mean that previous decisions were wrong. Times change, yet sadly in the Church we're often slow to make changes. We continue to do what used to work, wishing everything would go back to the way it was when our church was full and our ministries flourished, rather than stepping into God's call for us now.

The other reason I fail to act on the advice of others is far simpler. I struggle to do it because 'the spirit is willing, but the flesh is weak' (Matthew 26:41). Sermons and mentors prompt me to do something and I totally agree, but I don't actually get around to it. Moses could easily have agreed with Jethro, then in the busyness of the following weeks found it easier to just carry on. Delegation involves recruiting and training the right team and that takes time. It is quicker to just do it yourself.

For example, I know that it is far better to get a team of people giving the talk at church. But that involves planning the series, allotting the talks, reallocating the talks as people aren't available when I want them to be, talking to them about what they are speaking on, re-explaining what I mean by the series, talking their talk through with them and giving them feedback! It's quicker and easier to speak myself, as it involves much less organisation and preparation. We must not prevent others from flourishing in their calling because we are too busy to release them. A short-term win may be a much larger loss in the long term.

Constant complaining

If you remember, the complaints began even before the Israelites had crossed the Red Sea. The complaining only got worse as time passed and the people grew in number. Their initial hunger pangs led to God providing manna – literally lashings of bread from heaven. It was like wafers made with honey, lightly flavoured with coriander. But soon even that wasn't good enough and the complaints grew about the lack of a varied diet. Not only did they remember the pots of meat in Egypt, they now remembered fish, cucumbers, melons, leeks, onions and garlic (Numbers 11:5–6)!

Eventually, the Israelites' constant moaning made God angry. Moses plunged into self-pity. He had had enough. Leading the Israelites had become too much. He couldn't handle their complaints. In fact, he told God that he'd rather die (Numbers 11:15). God averted the crisis by appointing seventy elders to share Moses' leadership burden and by sending quail for the people to eat. But it was only a temporary reprieve.

Next, Moses' own sister and brother, Miriam and Aaron, turned on him (Numbers 12:1ff.). It began with a fair criticism. For some unknown reason, Moses had married a Cushite instead of an Israelite as he should have done. This definitely wasn't on God's wish list for him.[8] This allowed something deeper to surface. Seeds of comparison and resentment that had been dormant began to sprout. Aaron and Miriam began to question Moses' entire call to lead. They questioned why Moses was the main man, when God had equally spoken to the people through them.

Some complaints are justified or contain a valid observation. When I did a mission trip to Hong Kong many years ago, we had ten days of noodles for breakfast, lunch and dinner. I couldn't eat noodles for years afterwards, despite quite liking them beforehand. So I do have sympathy with the complaints about manna for every meal. But there is a difference between expressing a frustration and the life-draining effect of constant complaining.

---

8 Again, it is interesting to note that this clear departure from God's will didn't incur God's judgement, but we often think that the Old Testament is full of instant divine retribution.

Moses must have despaired over the moaning of the people. They were too thirsty, they were too hungry, they preferred Egypt, they were too scared … the list of their complaints was endless. And we are not so different in the Church today. There's always something to upset people! The worship is full of too many new songs or old songs, or both. The home groups are too big or too small, too frequent or infrequent. The leadership is changing too much and too quickly, or not enough. Sadly, complaining seems to be a part of human nature. It was true of the Israelites and is still the case today. We are meant to be recognised by our love, not our moaning, yet if we're honest, negativity can be more visible than love in some churches.

Rejected by those closest to him

Negativity can also rob us of love and we can end up writing people off. Aaron and Miriam's perspective of Moses became warped. They spotted a failing and this began a negative cycle. They start to see Moses as proud and arrogant when in fact, as the author of Numbers points out, he was the humblest man ever (Numbers 12:3). Leading us into these trains of thought has been a tactic employed by the devil since the earliest times. In the Garden of Eden, he raised doubts about God's motives and honesty, implying that God had misled Adam and Eve. We can so quickly feel unfairly treated and overlooked. I can think of a couple of friends in leadership who can totally write someone off if they let them down or upset them. They take against them and are suspicious of their character and motives from that moment onwards. We see this all the time in today's cancel culture. As Christians we need to make sure that we don't become prejudiced against someone because of a weakness or failing, let alone write them off. A critical view of someone can easily take root if we don't guard against it.

Pursuing God above all else

Moses led this enormous group of immensely fickle people for forty years, in a desert without a holiday – I honestly don't know how he did it! During this time, there were incredible highs with God. But they were often followed by crashing lows with the people.

After hearing the Ten Commandments, the people implored Moses to go and talk to God on their behalf because they were so scared (Exodus 20:18–19). Moses left the people at the foot of Mount Sinai, ascended into God's presence and received guidance for the whole future ordering of the people of Israel (Exodus 20 – 31). This took longer than they expected, so (always ones for melodrama) the Israelites concluded that Moses had gone off and left them. They decided that they would prefer to be like all the other nations, who had little gods they could see and touch and carry around with them. So they got Aaron to make a little god for them. In fairness it wasn't so little. It was a huge great golden calf. But it was tiny compared to the real God (Exodus 32:1ff.). They decided that this would cut out all the uncertainties associated with trusting an awesome, living God.

When Moses got back and found that they had built a golden calf, he and God were furious. God told Moses that he would honour the promise to give them the land of milk and honey, but they would have to go there without God. He said he was worried that he might end up destroying the Israelites because of their behaviour (Exodus 33:1–3). Moses was devastated. He knew that if God didn't go with them there would be no point in carrying on. Israel was marked out from the other nations because they were God's people. Moses pleaded with God on behalf of the Israelites and asked to be taught God's ways so that he would know him better (Exodus 33:12ff.).

We often worry about material things and then miss the spiritual point. We can put huge amounts of time, money and energy into an event and hardly any effort into praying for it. We can grieve the loss of something material or temporary and not notice that we've wandered away from God. Moses' concern was all about God and his glory. He didn't want to go anywhere without God's presence.

I know that in the past I've been more likely to beg God for success, happiness or comfort than pursue his glory. One of my favourite images from a worship song refers to the dedication of Solomon's Temple, when the weight of God's presence and glory was so great that they had to stop the service.[9] I've always loved the idea of having to stop a service because God's glory has fallen upon us and we simply can't continue. Often in Scripture we see that before discovering God's glory, people recognise the depths of their need for repentance and holiness. As for Solomon, I hope that God's glory will appear, but I wonder how willing I am to pursue this desire when it will involve personal cost, inconvenience and change.

The greatest passion of our faith should be living for God. We are called to deny ourselves, our wants and hopes, and take up our cross (Matthew 16:24). The Israelites, throughout their history, were meant to be a light to the Gentiles. They were supposed to model and reflect God and his values to the world. They never managed this. We, like them, are called to reflect God's presence and glory to those around us. In a dark and troubled world, people should be able to look at us and see glimpses of the light of Christ.

As Israel's leader, Moses was meant to reflect and model God to them. He was very much one of them; he was flawed, and failed throughout his life. Yet he was a leader who pointed them towards God. Throughout his life Moses messed up, lost faith and got angry, but after every stumble he went back to God, listened to him and returned to his calling as their leader. He is not recorded in Scripture as the perfect model of leadership. Instead, he illustrates that great leadership is not based on who the person is, but on who is with the person. Just as God was with Moses, God promises to

---

9   Matt Redman, 'Lord, let your glory fall' © 1998 Thankyou Music (Admin. by Capitol CMG Publishing).

be with us. Therefore, we all as normal, imperfect people can follow God's call to lead, because it isn't about us. It's all about God.

The Promised Land

The time had come to discover the Promised Land. God told Moses to send twelve spies, a representative from each tribe, to explore Canaan and report back (Numbers 13). They returned stunned by how incredible it was – the land was so fertile and the produce so abundant. It took two of them to carry a single cluster of grapes. But this was not the focus of their report. Instead, they spread doom and disaster, saying that the people were too strong and the Israelites couldn't win in a fight against them. Their consensus was that Israel had no hope of ever possessing the land of Canaan. Their fearmongering undermined the people's confidence and faith in God's promise.

However, two spies, Caleb and Joshua, had a totally different perspective. They said that Israel should go and take possession of the land, because they could, or rather God could. They were so passionate about obeying God that they argued with the people into the night. They ended up tearing their clothes, reassuring the people that they didn't need to be afraid, because God was with them (Numbers 14:1–38). But no one listened to them and the situation became so desperate that the others discussed stoning them. While all this was playing out, God called Moses to meet with him. He said that enough was enough. He would rather wipe the people out and begin again with just Moses (verse 12).

When Moses first received his call from God, he was reassured that God was with him. If Moses had measured himself against Pharaoh, the most powerful man of his day, there would have been no hope. However, if Moses measured Pharaoh against God there was equally no comparison. The twelve spies all saw the same things and recognised both the attractiveness of the place and the might of its inhabitants. Ten compared the might of the Canaanites to that of the Israelites. Two set it against God's might. It all came down to how people saw themselves in relation to God. As we will see later, the same situation would be repeated when it came to the Philistines and Goliath (spoiler alert!). As Christians, we need to see things from the perspective of God's power rather than our own.

God says that he's had enough

When God threatened to wipe the Israelites out, he couldn't actually have intended to destroy them. After all, he had promised after Noah that he would never wipe the people out again for their wickedness. So, what did his words mean?

It might have been another opportunity for Moses to be their representative. He repeatedly pleaded for the people and their salvation. Such was his love of them that he stood in the gap arguing their corner, just as Christ intercedes for us. It must have been so tempting for Moses not to advocate for them. He could easily have said, 'You know what, God, that's a great idea. They're doing my head in too. If it was just me and my family, that would be fantastic.'

Sadly, in a replay of what happened years before when Abraham interceded for Sodom and Gomorrah, many of the Israelites did die that day for their sin. But Moses' intercession rescued the majority. Not that their obedience to God lasted very long (Numbers 16).

Moses has had enough

A few chapters later, in Numbers 20, it was the first month of the final year in the desert. Most of those who originally escaped from Egypt had died, including Moses' beloved older sister Miriam. This new generation moaned just as much as their forebears, once again complaining about water. It's no wonder that Moses was at breaking point. He and Aaron fell flat on their faces before God. They encountered God's glory as he spoke to them. God sent them to gather the people before a rock and promised that water would gush forth. When everyone was assembled, Moses shouted at them before bashing the rock twice. The water appeared, but from that moment Moses lost his entry ticket to the Promised Land. God had told him simply to speak to the rock, but he had vented his anger, striking it twice, and this cost him dearly.

This seems totally unfair. The biblical examples we've looked at so far have got away with all sorts. Yet Moses gave in to his totally understandable frustration, bashed the rock against God's instructions and that marked the end of his leadership. You could be forgiven for thinking that a bit of angry rock-bashing wasn't that big a deal.

Well, God said that Moses did not trust in him enough to honour him as holy in the sight of the Israelites (Numbers 20:12). Moses rebuked the people: 'Listen, you rebels, must we bring you water out of this rock?' His words made two things apparent: he was putting himself in God's place as provider and he was standing in anger and judgement over the people. First, Moses made himself the focus of provision instead of God. Maybe, in some way, striking the rock indicated that Moses was the one with the power to provide instead of God. Or maybe he struck the rock because he was feeling sorry for himself. 'Poor Moses,' he was thinking. 'It's all down to you yet again.' As a church leader, I think that feeling is inevitable at times! These actions were out of character. Moses was described as the most humble man on the face of the earth, but here he was taking God's role upon himself.

Second, he struck the rock twice in anger. One hit might have been copying what God had called him to do on previous occasions to get water from rocks, but two hits suggests that it was more an act of aggression. We can understand that he was exasperated, but this was no excuse to fail as their leader. He was no longer one of the people interceding to God as one of them. He had taken judgement upon himself instead, when that should have been left to God.

This rock of Meribah had been a place of God's gracious provision. In the past, when the people had argued and complained, God gave them what they didn't deserve and provided water from this rock (Exodus 17). Moses turned it into a place of wrath, presenting God as short-tempered rather than merciful. This wasn't just about a leader losing his rag; this was spiritual. Water is spiritually significant, and it is perhaps not a coincidence that this incident comes after a chapter on the rituals for spiritual cleansing, including use of 'the water of cleansing' (Numbers 19:21).

Paul says in 1 Corinthians that the Israelites 'drank the same spiritual drink; for they drank from the spiritual rock that accompanied them, and that rock was Christ' (10:4). Moses' action twisted the truth about God as revealed most clearly in Christ. This may not be a concept we can easily understand, but it underlines that Moses' outburst had much greater significance and consequences than if it had just been a man losing his patience.

This is true of the actions of all of us as disciples, influencers and leaders. Christians, as demonstrated most powerfully by John the Baptist, are signposts to God and his character. We can either point towards God and who he is or away from him.

Sadly, I've talked to many people who have rejected Christ because of what they have seen expressed in his name by his supposed followers. That's something to stop and ponder. More and more people I meet say that they haven't given up on Jesus, but have given up on the Church. It used to sadden me when I went to summer Christian festivals and heard how the people local to the event regarded our behaviour. In the festival we would hear amazing and inspiring talks to encourage us in our witness to the world. But at the same time, festival-goers would nip offsite to Tesco between meetings and cut people up in the car park and be rude to people at the checkouts. Locals used to comment that they preferred the secular festivals.

When Christians behave like that, I'm not surprised people are disinterested in our faith. Rightly, leaders carry even more responsibility. They are in a greater position to influence people's understanding and experience of God. People absorb more from what they see and what is left unsaid than from what is preached and taught (James 3:1). Every part of our lives needs to reflect Jesus, both what we say and what we do.

As I hope this book makes patently clear, God doesn't expect us to get everything right. It is pretty much guaranteed that we will make mistakes and let God, ourselves and others down. We should, however, be aware of our weaknesses and address rather than excuse them.

When I was interviewed for a place at theological college – or the vicar factory – I was asked a question that really annoyed me. The interviewer asked me what I would do if everything was going wrong in ministry. Would I be most likely to take some of the collection money, hit the communion wine, go off with a choir boy or have a fling with the churchwarden's wife? I was appalled. What kind of immoral, liberal attitude did he have? I barely covered my disdain and said something about how I would pray and look to Jesus. But over years of ministry, I recognise more and more what an important issue it was to face. I need to know myself and recognise where I am weakest and most vulnerable.

I have seen several churches decimated by their leader having an affair. I know at least two where financial impropriety has been a real problem. On reflection, I don't think the interviewer went broad enough with his question, and I would add another category: am I liable to start controlling people and the church? Increasingly I see more and more churches where the leader bullies and controls. 'Coercive behaviour' is a concept I'd never heard of a few years ago and now I hear it all too frequently.

Abuses of power are less black and white than sexual misconduct. They can easily be put down to personality clashes or pursuing

God's call even when it's unpopular. But anger and control can crush and ruin lives in an insidious way. People are left doubting themselves and God. They can leave the Church because, for them, it's a place of pain. God's nature and character become twisted, as he can be dragged down with a poorly behaved leader.

We see this confusion playing out here with Moses, the humblest man, presuming to stand in God's place. I regularly need to revisit that question posed by my interviewer. I suggest we all do. We all need to be aware of how we can react when we're under pressure.

Journey's end

After this failure Moses went on to lead the people for some time to come. He set everything in place for the Promised Land. He finished teaching the people how to set up healthy societal structures. He organised the division of the land and trained up his successor, Joshua.

We see many parallels between the rescue from slavery God brought through Moses and what was to come with Jesus. There's so much more that could be written about his leadership in the desert. But I think the best way to leave the story of Moses is in the same way it is left in the Bible. He may not have got to enter the Promised Land, but he would be remembered as follows:

> Since then, no prophet has risen in Israel like Moses, whom the LORD knew face to face, who did all those signs and wonders the LORD sent him to do in Egypt – to Pharaoh and to all his officials and to his whole land. For no one has ever shown the mighty power or performed the awesome deeds that Moses did in the sight of all Israel.
> (Deuteronomy 34:10–12)

Quite impressive after that dodgy start!

Part 3

THE TALE OF TWO KINGS

5
Saul

Time for a king

Moses was succeeded as leader of Israel by Joshua. After Joshua came a series of judges. They were a mixture of triumphs and failures. Ultimately everyone did what was right in their own eyes and the Israelites decided that having an imperfect judge ruling over them didn't work. They yearned for something better. By the end of this sorry period, Israel was desperate just to be like everyone else around them and have a king (1 Samuel 8). Their whole identity and mission was supposed to be rooted in the very fact that they had God and weren't like the other nations. But they missed this point.

Samuel, who was God's mouthpiece at the time, warned them against appointing a king. He listed many reasons that should have won them round: a king would take their sons off to battle, he would make their daughters work for him and he would collect taxes! The people were unmoved. They still wanted a king. So in response, God said, 'Give them what they want.'

Heart not height

There just so happened to be a man at that time who was without equal among the Israelites (1 Samuel 9). That was especially true if you measured him on height alone – which at five feet eight and a half inches tall, I tend not to do! This guy Saul was a head taller than everyone else. In a time of kings leading their people into battle, the stature and bearing of the king were important attributes.

Saul's regal rise from peasanthood began one ordinary day. Saul's dad had lost his donkeys and he was sent to look for them. He and a servant travelled so far in their donkey-hunting, Saul began to worry that his dad would think he was lost. The servant suggested they seek the help of a wise, local man of God. According to the servant, this man was a prophet of God and everything he said came true. Saul wasn't convinced. After a little persuasion from the servant, they set out to find the prophet called Samuel.

They ended up bumping into Samuel and asking him where to find the prophet. God had already told Samuel that he was about to meet Saul. He'd even revealed to him that Saul would be Israel's first king. Samuel introduced himself and asked Saul and his servant to stay until the following day. He promised that the next morning he would tell Saul all that was in Saul's heart. Samuel offhandedly informed them that their donkeys were fine and then told them that all of Israel's desires were focused on his dad's family. This made no sense to Saul, as he was from the smallest, least-popular tribe.[1]

For characters in the Bible, often the first scene they appear in, or the first thing they say, reveals something of their nature. Saul entered the stage talking about donkeys and we quickly discover that he had far less spiritual awareness than his servant. His focus was, and would remain, on material things and outward appearances. His servant dropped in that everything Samuel said came true, but Saul paid no attention.

Samuel told Saul that he would reveal all that was in his heart. That must have been both attractive and terrifying in equal measure. How often do we want God to reveal things about us and how often do we run away from such revelation? One of my favourite prayers in Anglican liturgy is the Collect for Purity. It

---

1 If you want to know why, it's all down to a terrible incident that took place in Judges 19 and 20. It's worth a read, but it's not an easy one.

begins, 'Almighty God, unto whom all hearts be open, all desires known, and from whom no secrets are hid.' Nothing is hidden from God, so we have nothing to fear from his knowledge of us. Also, it means that God doesn't make mistakes when he calls us to something.

Saul's response to his call was that he came from an insignificant family. But a sense of insignificance is no barrier to God. Still, though, if Saul didn't get past this struggle with insignificance it would be his downfall. This theme is at the heart of Saul's story. Samuel didn't address Saul's concerns, but instead whisked him and his servant off to be guests of honour at a banquet. After the banquet he took them back to his home and spent much of the night on the roof talking to Saul. What did they talk about? Did he tell him *all* that was in his heart? Annoyingly it is another of those moments when the Bible leaves us wondering.

Anointing

The next morning Samuel sent the servant on ahead so that he and Saul were alone. He gave Saul a message from God. The biblical account is very understated: 'Then Samuel took a flask of olive oil and poured it on Saul's head and kissed him, saying, "Has not the LORD anointed you ruler over his inheritance?"' (1 Samuel 10:1). Any one of those things would have been a big deal, but the anointing must have left the biggest mark – quite literally.

When I was ordained a bishop, a couple of people warned me that when the archbishop anoints bishops at their consecration, he doesn't hold back. I was expectant, but in no way prepared for quite how much oil he would pour on my head. It just kept on and on coming and for the rest of the day I could feel and smell it. That was only a small jug – Saul got the whole flask. I was interviewed as soon as I left the service and asked what had been the most memorable part of the event. I blurted out that there was so much oil. I then tried to make a more profound comment about my need for an abundance of the Spirit in my leadership as a bishop. The abundance of the oil flowing over my hair and clothes was a good visual representation of my prayer for God's Spirit to empower my leadership. God's call on our lives isn't begrudging or half-hearted. It is abundant and at times can feel socially awkward. Even Saul couldn't have failed to realise something special was going on.

Life change

Samuel got practical and reassured Saul about all the things that were worrying him (1 Samuel 10). He told Saul that he would meet two men who would tell him where the donkeys were and that his dad was concerned for his well-being. Next, Saul would meet three men who would give him bread. Finally, Saul would run into a worship event, where he would be overwhelmed by the Holy Spirit and changed into a different person. In fact, as soon as 'Saul turned to leave Samuel, God changed Saul's heart' (1 Samuel 10:9). Everything then happened just as Samuel predicted. When people saw Saul prophesying, they were shocked. He was pretty much the last person they expected to become a prophet.

God placed an incredible call on Saul's life, but he was also interested in the details. First and foremost, the donkeys were fine. Second, Saul and his servant had run out of food, so God met that need too. But, as Jesus said, 'Man shall not live on bread alone' (Matthew 4:4). He also needed to encounter God and be changed. He did exactly this. Yet even with a heart that had been transformed, he still faced some of the same struggles and weaknesses he always had.

It's the same for us. When we become a Christian God gives us a new heart, but there isn't a hard reset button for our behaviour and attitudes. Those things take time, perhaps a lifetime or longer. Paul talked about 'the flesh'.[2] By this he meant our old thought patterns and desires, our default and even subconscious human reactions. Paul knew that even though in Christ we are newly created, our thoughts and feelings still need ongoing work. In this story we see that Saul was changed, but he still had to choose to trust God rather than go back to old beliefs and behaviours. This struggle within Saul became increasingly apparent.

The first hint is given when he returned home and was challenged by his uncle about what took so long. He told him that they went to Samuel, and knowing who Samuel was (unlike Saul), the uncle asked what Samuel had said. Saul gave him the bare practical details, telling him about the donkeys but leaving out the whole 'you're anointed to be king' prophecy. Saul didn't own up to his incredible experience of God. Perhaps he was embarrassed or confused, or was trying to work out for himself what it all meant. We can be the same. It is so easy to clam up about our faith, or what we think God is doing in our lives.

A young businessman used to be too embarrassed to talk about church. If people asked about his weekend, he would brush over the church bit. One day he felt convicted that if he wouldn't even talk about church, he had no chance of ever sharing his faith. He intentionally began to include church in his conversations. He'd say that he'd had a great time having food with friends on Saturday, church had been really exciting, and then he'd gone for a nice walk on Sunday afternoon. He'd describe church in an unexpected way each time it came up. Soon, people began to pick up on the fact that he'd referred to church as 'exciting', 'emotional' or 'challenging'. In no time, they were asking to come with him to experience this impactful church.

---

2 For example, in Romans 8:5 the Greek word *sarx* means 'flesh'. Somewhat unhelpfully if you have an older NIV Bible translation, it is translated as 'sinful nature'. The latest version has corrected it to 'flesh'.

I know it can be easier to hold back on talking about Jesus or what God is doing in our lives for fear of being seen as weird. But if we aren't honest about our faith, that will have a negative effect in the long term. The people around us will never understand what our Christian faith means to us if we reluctantly give them the bare bones. If we tell them nothing of the substance and content, the joy and the hope of our faith, then they will never understand our love for God and our desire to be faithful in our walk with him.

The big reveal

Samuel summoned the whole of Israel to Mizpah. He declared that God was their king, but that they had rejected him for a human version and God would give them what they desired. They were instructed to line up by tribes and clans. I picture this as being much like the big reveal in a TV production. First, Samuel (an ancient Ant and Dec, if you will) announces which tribe the king will be from. He probably drags it out by slowly revealing which tribes *haven't* been selected, each one shuffling backwards with their heads hanging in disappointment. The drama builds as he whittles it down to the tribes of Judah, Reuben and Benjamin. Everyone is guessing which of Reuben and Judah it is, since it can't possibly be the disgraced and tiny tribe of Benjamin. The audience gasps and the ancient Reddit thread blows up when they reveal it is the tribe of Benjamin.

Next, Samuel announces that the king will be from the clan of Matri. I imagine a spotlight resting on their cluster as family after family is dismissed until they are down to just Kish's family. Then comes the grand finale: who is it going to be? Samuel's voice echoes across the gathered multitude, 'The first king of Israel is … [cue drum roll] … Saul!' The spotlight moves to … Hang on, he isn't there! Cut to an awkward commercial break.

Fantasy TV show aside, they genuinely couldn't find him. They ended up having to ask God where he was. God told them he was hiding with the baggage. Sure enough, there he was. Their new king. His head poking out from behind a donkey. God had already done so much for Saul, and what happened? Terrified at the enormity of his calling, Saul hid with the donkeys and bags. It is so easy for us to go back to the old familiar ways and places. We might not even like them, but they feel safe. We can have amazing experiences of God, but if we don't allow God to help us change our attitudes, beliefs and behaviours, we can easily slip back to where we started.

This can take many forms. It can be returning to what has been a source of comfort or made us feel better in the past, like food or alcohol. It can be finding our worth in achievements, chasing after another qualification or title to make us feel worthwhile. It can be looking for a relationship or a hook-up to make us feel attractive. It can be the feeling of safety that being in control brings. God is calling us out of the old ways that ultimately left us trapped. He's calling us to the wide-open spaces of freedom.

Dealing with opposition

Despite the shaky start, there were some positive signs. Saul went back to his home town of Gibeah, accompanied by good, 'valiant men whose hearts God had touched' (1 Samuel 10:26). At that time some people rose up against him, asking, 'How can this fellow save us?' Amazingly, Saul ignored them and stayed silent. He showed restraint. For a while he seemed to go back to normal life on his dad's farm, despite having been chosen as king (1 Samuel 11:5).

One day he got back from ploughing and heard about a gruesome threat to gouge out the right eyes of the men from an Israelite town called Jabesh Gilead. God powerfully moved him to a righteous anger, and with no thought for himself or his reputation, Saul called on the whole people of Israel to rescue the men of Jabesh Gilead. This is one of the few moments when Saul was being led by God as he led the people.

Saul's mission was successful. Some people suggested that his critics should be put to death, but Saul stopped this from happening. He also gave all the credit for the victory to God and took none for himself (1 Samuel 11:12–13). The people of Israel ended up worshipping God at Gilgal. Samuel gave a rousing retirement speech about fearing and serving God. There were even divine pyrotechnics – well, thunder and rain – and understandable awe of the Lord (1 Samuel 12:18).

The thing is, though, that question – 'How can this fellow save us?' – wasn't so stupid. The truth was that Saul couldn't save them. If only they and Saul had recognised that only God could save them, all would have been well.

The way leaders respond to their critics can be even more significant than how they handle their supporters. All too often leaders become defensive or aggressive. They can end up becoming increasingly controlling, without seeing how bad and manipulative their behaviour is. This can be the result of surrounding themselves with people who agree with them and won't challenge them.

In leadership we need to be as self-aware as possible. In fact, the most experienced person I know in making church leadership appointments says that self-awareness is the most important leadership quality. It's good to have people who love us pointing out the things we aren't aware of. But if we truly want to understand ourselves better, we also need the input of those who don't agree with us.

Self-promotion

So far so good for Saul. He rescued Jabesh Gilead, gave God the credit and didn't lash out against his critics. At this point, he was still young and would go on to reign for forty-two years (1 Samuel 13:1). In his next move as king, Saul chose 3,000 troops and sent the rest of his army home. This would turn out to be a bad call. He kept 2,000 soldiers for himself and gave 1,000 to his son Jonathan – not the fairest division. Jonathan mounted an attack on an enemy outpost of Philistines. But rather than acknowledge the work of his son, Saul had it announced that he had led the attack.

If he'd had X (the social media platform formerly known as Twitter), Saul would have been all over it with @tallkingsaul proclaiming his achievements. It's concerning how many leaders feel the need to tell the world of their every success. It is not just US presidents, industry leaders, those in government – it's church leaders too. It's so easy to find significance in the attention, applause or 'likes' of others.

In contrast, a while ago I was with one of the most humble retired leaders I know. He had just returned from a celebration event for one of the greatest modern-day missionaries. I asked his connection with her. He said that as a young woman she had been in a Bible study group with him. It was his wife who added that it was through that group the woman had become a Christian. In twenty-five years of knowing him I had never heard him refer to this connection once. He never claimed any part of her success as his own. He doesn't seek man's accolades, but is happy to serve for God's pleasure and applause alone. I question myself before sharing anything on social media. Am I sharing stories that speak of God's goodness or am I really after affirmation?

Taking things into his own hands

Having claimed Jonathan's attack as his own, Saul then called all the men back to Gilgal, presumably including those he'd already sent away. All his bragging had thoroughly provoked the Philistines. In response they started to assemble, growing greater and greater in number. Their army became so vast, they had 3,000 enemy chariots, 6,000 charioteers, and soldiers as numerous as the sand on the seashore. (Wasn't comparing the numbers of people with grains of sand meant to be Israel's thing from God's promise to Abraham?) The Israelites were understandably scared and many ran away. Some hid in bushes, caves, pits and cisterns (these were tanks for storing water rather than just the backs of toilets). Those who were left with Saul were literally shaking with fear.

Samuel told Saul to wait seven days, after which he would come and perform the appointed pre-battle sacrifice at Gilgal. Making this sacrifice was key, because it dedicated the Israelites afresh to God, placing their trust in him as *his* army. It could only be done by a priest or prophet. Each day would have been more distressing than the last as the Philistine army grew, and more and more Israelites ran away.

On the seventh day, the Israelites were down to very few men. This was Saul's first real battle, his moment to shine, and it was falling apart before it even started. Saul lost his nerve. He decided that they had to go into battle before there was no one left in his army. He knew he was supposed to wait for Samuel to offer a sacrifice, but instead he took matters into his own hands and offered the sacrifice himself. Under God's law Saul was not qualified to do this, but desperate times caused him to decide to take desperate measures. He might have thought he was doing the right thing. He wasn't. As soon as he finished the sacrifice, Samuel arrived. Such annoying timing.

Do you ever feel that God is a bit like Samuel? He doesn't seem to show up when you need him. As someone once said, God is almost always nearly late. Mary and Martha would have had sympathy with that view (John 11:1–43). In spite of their pleading, Jesus took three days to come when their brother Lazarus was sick. He wasn't even very far away. But he was too late and Lazarus died. Martha and Mary both said to Jesus, 'If you had been here, my brother would not have died' (verses 21 and 32). This thinking is only a small step from believing that God doesn't show up on time and can't be relied on.

We have some friends who are amazing pastors. They are the kind of people who, when they start asking you questions, you know something is going on. At one point we were talking about the setbacks of ministry and they challenged me about whether I engage with disappointment. I said I thought I did, but they pushed me on it. What unfolded was that if something didn't happen as I had hoped, I would just shrug my shoulders and move on. At the same time, I also didn't ostensibly take other people's pain on myself in pastoral situations, so I could handle quite a large pastoral load. My friends pointed out that these two characteristics were subtly eroding my faith. Although everything appeared good on the surface, subconsciously disappointment was taking root. Contending with trauma in other people's lives was leaving me with an insidious sense that God was not entirely good and couldn't be relied on.

It's all too easy to stop trusting in God and start taking things into our own hands. We keep up an appearance of spirituality while secretly building in back-up plans. We need to bring our disappointments and doubts to God and work them through in the way that is most helpful for us. We are all different and God will meet each of us where we are.

Saul can't carry on

Samuel arrived and was hit by the smell of barbecue. He asked Saul what he'd done. Saul's defence was twofold. First, he tried to shift the blame on to anyone but himself. He reminded Samuel that he didn't turn up on time, the Philistines were gathering and his people were scattering. Second, he attempted to justify his actions as spiritual and holy. He argued that someone needed to seek God's favour and no one else was available! Samuel rebuked Saul and told him that Israel could have been his kingdom, but because of his disobedience, God had sought out someone else after his own heart. His time as king was essentially over.

Saul did everything he could to avoid taking responsibility for his actions. In truth, he panicked. He was led by the men's fear and was scared of failure. He was more concerned about himself and his leadership than God's will and God's leadership.

If we're honest, God's decision to end Saul's leadership seems a bit harsh. Saul was under extreme pressure, facing his own death and that of his remaining men. Others have done far worse and been trusted with leadership rather than lost it. Yet Saul's story is about more than just him. He was Israel's first king. Until this point, Israel had looked to the might of God rather than that of their warrior king like other nations. Saul's actions affected the faith of God's people. A people who were meant to draw attention to God, not themselves.

While we may never fully understand or know the whole story, Saul's rejection seems to be about his heart and motivation rather than a single incident. In the few glimpses we have of his behaviour, he consistently worried more about people's view of him than people's view of God. Faith doesn't need to be huge or even that consistent. As we saw with Abraham, his faith was somewhat sketchy, but it was faith nonetheless.

Saul's actions contrasted sharply with those of Gideon (Judges 6 and 7). We touched on this story in the call of Moses and saw that Gideon was not a brave man. When God called him, he was hiding from the Midianites, grinding his grain in a winepress. He was terrified. He tried to resist God's call, until finally he ran out of options.

God commissioned Gideon to fight the Midianites with a scratch army. But then somehow more than 30,000 men turned up at Harad to fight with him. That had to be a confidence boost! Worryingly for Gideon, God made him send loads of them away. The numbers of fighting men went from 32,000 to 10,000 and finally to a paltry 300. It was a bonkers plan! But Gideon obeyed God, sending huge batches of fighters home as he was told, until his army was so small he had no chance (humanly speaking). However, with God, victory was certain and victory was what he got.

Gideon struggled to have faith, yet he journeyed with God, bringing his doubts before God so that he could be reassured. Gideon was young, with no title or official position; he was simply called by God to lead. In contrast, Saul had official position and status. He had the authority of being a king.

Saul's actions were also very different from Samuel's. Samuel knew what it was to have the Philistines looming down on him (1 Samuel 7:5ff.). One day, way before Saul was on the scene, Samuel called the people of Israel to a gathering at Mizpah. Mid-worship service, the Philistines began to close in and attack them. Samuel didn't focus on the enemy and his immediate circumstances, but rather on God. He wasn't led by the people's fear; he spoke into it and called their attention back to God. He told them not to stop crying out to God in repentance. Meanwhile he offered a sacrifice and interceded for them. The Philistines continued to draw closer, but at the last possible moment, God threw them into confusion and they were defeated without the Israelites even raising a weapon.

When Saul was told that his reign was as good as over, his reaction was revealing. He certainly didn't tweet about it! No, he went and counted his men. When we are told off or feel bad, often the last thing we want to do is face up to it. It's so tempting to try to make ourselves feel better: 'I may have messed that up, but at least my church is a decent size' or 'I may have messed that up, but I've still got lots of Instagram followers'. Comparison with others is never the answer. The way forward is to draw close to God. We need to look to him for comfort and fresh reassurance.

Who's taking the lead?

Saul may have got it wrong, but his son Jonathan got it right when he declared, 'Nothing can hinder the LORD from saving, whether by many or by few' (1 Samuel 14:6). Jonathan understood that it wasn't about the size of the army, but who the army belonged to.

Once again Jonathan took pre-emptive action against the Philistines, just as at the first battle when he launched the attack and Saul took the credit.[3] You might think that Jonathan was a reckless troublemaker. He was the one who caused the Philistines to muster at Gilgal and now he was at it again. However, unlike with his father, God was clearly in the forefront of Jonathan's mind. He recognised that God could act on their behalf and that 'the LORD has given them into the hand of Israel' (1 Samuel 14:12). More significantly, he referred to the Philistines as 'those uncircumcised men' (verse 6). This was more than just an anatomical or cultural comment. Circumcision was the sign that the people of Israel were God's chosen people. The Philistines were not.

Jonathan and his armour-bearer killed 'twenty men in an area of about half an acre' (verse 14). Don't you just love the detail? This isn't some legend or made-up story. This is an account of what actually happened. God created a panic in the middle of the Philistines, and they started dispersing, all because of two men and God. Around this time, Saul picked up on the disturbance. He had apparently learned something about being in God's army from his past experiences, because this time he called for the priest and the ark of the covenant (1 Samuel 14:15ff.). He was going to get the priest to seek God's direction, but as he was organising this the chaos in the Philistine camp grew, the pressure mounted and he told the priest not to bother and rushed into battle.

---

3 Last time it was 1 Samuel 13:3ff. and this is 14:1ff.

So far we've seen two aspects to Jonathan's character: he recognised that the battle belonged to the Lord and he wasn't afraid to make bold, maybe even reckless, moves against the enemy. Saul seemed to lack both these attributes. He was more panicked than bold, and he struggled to recognise God's leading and authority. There were moments, such as here, where he made faltering steps to look to God and his leadership. Saul recognised that he needed God's help but, as soon as the Philistine panic increased, he either thought he needed to act quickly or decided it was easy enough for him to just get on with it without God's input.

Sometimes we ignore God because we are in a panic. Sometimes we neglect God because things seem to be going our way and we don't feel the need for his input. As followers of God, and disciples, we need to learn to deepen our trust and dependence on God, in the good times and bad. We need to choose to consistently pause and turn our attention to him and his will, until it becomes our default.

It gets worse...

Another day another disaster for Saul (1 Samuel 14:24). He had made the mistake of issuing a somewhat rash unilateral declaration. Earlier, when it looked as though they were in for an easy victory, Saul had declared that no one was to eat any food until it was all over. Not only that, but anyone who did eat would be cursed.

Bold statements can have the appearance of strong, decisive leadership, but they can just as easily be self-centred or insecure attempts to look like a great leader. Saul's declaration focused on himself: 'Cursed be anyone who eats food before evening comes, before *I* have avenged *myself* on *my* enemies!' (1 Samuel 14:24, my italics). Mature leadership should not be about getting noticed, but about leading your people well. Leaders need to be decisive but not impetuous. Occasionally, quick decisions must be made, but more often better decisions take time, consideration and consultation.

Good leadership is about making good decisions, not quick or big ones. Saul's statement wasn't thought through. It was an attention-grabbing act that, as we will see, had dire consequences. Israel would live with the effects for years to come. Saul's vow distracted from dealing with the Philistines and, as a result, they continued to be plagued by them for years to come.

...and worse

As the Israelite army walked through some woods, they passed lots of honey (1 Samuel 14:25–27). They were tired and hungry. This would have been just the sugar and morale boost they needed. Jonathan hadn't heard about his dad's embargo on food, so he used his staff as a honey dipper. Immediately his eyes brightened. Everyone else must have known Saul's rule, because they passed by famished. When the day's battle was over, the soldiers were so weak, exhausted and hungry that they desperately started ripping at the plundered flocks and ate with the blood still in them, breaking a basic Jewish law about not eating food with blood in it. Saul saw the problem and brilliantly (and unusually) intervened, organising for them to have kosher meat. He even followed up by building an altar to the Lord. Saul was learning how important it was to follow God's law, but it was all a bit too little too late.

Next, Saul ordered a night raid to finish off the Philistines. The people seemed beyond caring; their response was, 'Whatever!' It was the priest who told him to hang on and check with God. Saul did, but God didn't respond. In a rare moment of discernment, Saul realised that God's silence meant there was some unresolved sin between Israel and God.[4] He called on God to show him where the sin lay, then moseyed off with Jonathan, waiting to hear from God.

---

4 In Isaiah 59:2 it says: 'But your iniquities have separated you from your God; your sins have hidden his face from you, so that he will not hear.'

Presumably Saul assumed there was no chance the sin would be with him or his son, but quickly Jonathan was singled out for eating the honey. He knew his dad was totally wrong to stop the men eating and to have made an oath about it, but an oath was still an oath. So when the lot pointed to him, and Saul asked what he had done, his instant response was, 'I tasted a little honey with the end of my staff. And now I must die!' (1 Samuel 14:43).

Saul took that oath seriously and then doubled down making another before God. He recklessly said that God should deal with him so severely if Jonathan didn't die. This wasn't a demonstration of great passion for holiness. Saul didn't want to lose face, so stuck to his word. At this point, the soldiers rose up and stood against Saul. They pointed out the stupidity of his actions and rescued Jonathan.

So, what was the consequence of this sad interlude? Jonathan and the men must have lost, rather than gained, respect for Saul. Most significantly, this interruption meant that they didn't finish their pursuit of the Philistines. Saul's arrogant declaration that no one would eat until they'd finished the job had the reverse effect. Instead of hurrying the end of the conflict, Jonathan's honey eating interrupted the battle and the Philistines lived on to plague the Israelites for years to come.

I wonder how often my attention is too much on myself to the detriment of God's plans and kingdom and the people I lead. I recently heard about a church leader having a go at the sound operator from the front of a crowded church because the microphone wasn't working properly. He was upset, because it looked unprofessional, and I guess he felt that it hindered his performance that morning. However, I think that the unprofessionalism the congregation observed was not that of the sound operator. Sadly, most of us who lead have made many similar mistakes.

I have been ordained for more than twenty-five years and have spent a lot of time working with the diocesan staff. One of the things that shocked me most when I became a bishop was how often people deferred to me for decisions in meetings. For example, before someone begins training to get ordained, they go through a period of discernment, with all sorts of reading, meetings and interviews. In our diocese at least five people must agree that they are ready to go to the formal national selection residential. But before they can actually go, a bishop has to meet with them and give approval. They have been through a rigorous process with skilled and trained people prior to seeing me. It would take a lot for me to go against their wisdom, but I also realise there may well come a time when I should. I am willing to carry the ultimate responsibility in leadership decisions such as these, but only because I am working alongside wise people. I have seen far too many occasions where decisions that are rushed or lack any kind of process end badly.

Destruction

Although Saul's kingship was essentially already over, God still had work for him to do. Samuel gave Saul explicit directions about what had to happen next (1 Samuel 15). At times Liz asks me to do something, and I half listen and remember the gist of the request. It doesn't normally end well. Sadly, I don't seem to learn! Saul may have had the same problem. He certainly couldn't say that God didn't give him clear instructions. He was told in no uncertain terms to attack the Amalekites and destroy everything. And by 'everything', God meant men and women, children and infants, cattle and sheep, camels and donkeys. After the battle, Saul could perhaps be forgiven for missing the pet dogs, cats and rabbits, but nothing else.

In many ways it would be nice if these instructions had been a bit vaguer, since it's such a horrific concept. The idea that God might have wanted him to kill anyone, let alone explicitly include children, is never going to sit comfortably with us. It was a common part of warfare in ancient times to annihilate everything. But the concept of annihilation, or *herem*, isn't quite that simple. The Hebrew word *herem* refers to something being utterly destroyed, but it doesn't always mean this. It can be understood as separating something from God's presence.

It is worth noting that, at this point in history, the salvation story is being lived out and expressed through a particular people group. God is seeking to establish a kingdom of justice and mercy and grace that is completely counter-cultural. This means, at many points in the Old Testament, orders for *herem* are about removing the identity of a people whose culture and practices are abhorrent to God's kingdom – like, for example, if they sacrifice children. The command for *herem* may in part be a demonstration of the fact that the consequence of sin is death. Therefore, there was a reason for the command of *herem*. But even if we are beginning to understand it, we may not find this an acceptable justification to our modern ears.[5]

However, with the Amalekites there was a particular reason. During the exodus from Egypt, they had followed the Israelite refugees and preyed on the weak and vulnerable. They had taken out those who lagged behind: women, children and the sick. Back then God had encouraged the Israelites, stating that the Amalekites would be dealt with severely (Deuteronomy 25:17–19). In part, God's command at this point was an attempt to avoid greater bloodshed later, when they would rally and fight again, and the violence would continue to escalate over generations, with many more dying.

---

5 This is a really difficult and emotive topic for us to begin to understand. A really helpful and much fuller unpacking can be found in Helen Paynter's excellent book *God of Violence Yesterday, God of Love Today?* (Oxford: Bible Reading Fellowship, 2019).

Saul's final act of disobedience

Saul went out to battle against the Amalekites (1 Samuel 15:4). Clearly some time had passed, as his army was 210,000 strong. The Israelites won a decisive victory, but they spared the king and any sheep and cattle worth keeping. Last time, Samuel had arrived to the smell of a barbecue; this time it was the sound of a farmyard. When he arrived, there was no sign of Saul (1 Samuel 15:12). Saul was off building a monument in his own honour before leaving for Gilgal.

Eventually they caught up with each other and Saul greeted Samuel cheerily, declaring that he had done everything God asked. Samuel pointed out the slightly contradictory sound of bleating and mooing. Saul, as always, began to blame his soldiers and gave a pseudo-spiritual justification for his disobedience. He countered Samuel with something along the lines of, 'What could be better than delaying the destruction of the best animals for a big sacrifice to God? In fact, we thought you could do it, Samuel, since you've told me off before for doing sacrifices before you arrive.'

Little did Saul know that God had already told Samuel all about it before he got there. Although by then you'd think Saul would have guessed. When Samuel had heard about Saul's disobedience, he spent the whole night crying out to God before getting up early to visit the battlefield.

Let's take a moment for Samuel here – wasn't he amazing? God told him that Saul had let him down again, and Samuel's response was to spend the whole night troubled and crying out to the Lord. Before Saul was made king, Samuel had consistently said that God shouldn't give the people a king. He could justifiably have taken great delight in Saul's downfall. Instead, he interceded all night. He prayed for the Lord's anointed king, even when he'd lost his anointing. In fact, so great was Samuel's concern for Saul that God was forced to tell him just to get over it and get on with it (1 Samuel 16:1). What a challenge!

If we are honest, many Christians find it far easier to spot and judge other people's sin. Some of us may also have a tendency to want God to treat them as we perceive they deserve. It's a kind of warped sense of justice. It is this kind of thinking that Jesus was challenging when he talked about removing the plank from your own eye to remove the speck from someone else's.

How do you get a heart like Samuel's for those who are disappointing and hard work? I think one way is by praying for them. Rather than moaning about them to others, we need to talk to God about them. And as we pray, we need to recognise that no matter how bad their behaviour is, God still loves them.

Years ago, I heard a brilliant speaker at a youth event talk about her sister – let's call her Anna. At secondary school, Anna started being left out by a group of friends in her class. They formed a group called 'Leave out Anna'. It got so bad that in the end Anna would eat her lunch in a toilet cubicle. Somehow, despite them picking on her, she would pray for them. She also continued to be kind to them. She wouldn't blank them and still said hello to them. They continued to be mean to her and she continued to pray for them as, on and off, this carried on for a couple of years. Then one summer holiday, one of the girls wrote to her. In the letter she said that she was so sorry for how they had treated her. She said she didn't know why they had ever started being mean to her, and that it was nothing she had done.

Miraculously, over time, they created a strong friendship group, and Anna's friends attended Christian youth events for the first time, to support Anna in her faith. They ended up as house mates, bridesmaids at each other's weddings and helping each other when their parents were unwell, and they remain the best of friends to this day. Now, I know that not every story ends so positively. In fact if I didn't know Anna's sister myself it could sound too good to be true. But it is true, and Anna beautifully demonstrated two things: our actions are not determined by those of other people and we don't have to reciprocate their unloving attitudes. We should pray for people no matter what.

Shame versus repentance

Even when Samuel confronted Saul for a second time about his disobedience in saving the plunder and the king, Saul denied it and made excuses (1 Samuel 15:20). Finally, Saul confessed that he had sinned and asked Samuel to forgive him. He also asked Samuel to come back with him so they could worship God. Is this an encouraging sign? Samuel turned down the invitation and went to leave, but Saul grabbed hold of him and ripped his robe in an attempt to stop him. Saul's true motive was revealed here: he didn't want to go back without Samuel and be shamed before the elders.

Even after Samuel emphasised God's rejection of Saul, Saul was worried about how it would look. He didn't want people to know. These were the same people he had consistently tried to keep happy, even if it meant disobeying God. It was far more important that God went with him than Samuel did. He hadn't learned from the example of Moses.

I know that God loves me no matter what and will always forgive me, but people are less loving and forgiving. Additionally, the judgement of others is more apparent and has a more immediate effect on my life. God promises to be with me always, I know he won't walk out on me, but my friends and people at church so easily can. On the one hand I try to live and act following and obeying God. I want my life to be lived out in front of the one who matters. But on the other hand I recognise that I can be like Saul. Distress and concern about what others think can often run deeper than my repentance. When I'm convicted of getting it wrong, I so easily try to shift the blame. I can be upset by the accusations, or at being found out, but I am not necessarily deeply repentant. It is important to note that sorrow is not the same as repentance.[6] Sin – which literally means 'missing the mark' – matters. I need to learn to take it as seriously as God does, or in fact Samuel does. Self-pity or even sorrow is not enough. I need to repent, literally turn away from my sin.

Sadly, I often see shame and sorrow rather than genuine repentance in relationships. I know too many church leaders who have messed up, whether it's by having an actual affair or overstepping the line relationally or pastorally. At least a couple were devastated by what happened, but then over time it became apparent that the devastation was more about the shame, or loss of their position and standing, than a real repentance. They didn't grapple with their behaviour in repentance. Like Saul, it was about shame more than repentance.

This is in sharp contrast to one priest I know. He was at a low point in his own emotional health and got too involved with someone he was caring for pastorally. I don't know exactly what happened, although he explicitly gave me permission to ask anything about it. He never dreamed that it could happen to him, but his life had become compartmentalised, and he ended up compromised without even realising it. When it was discovered, he said, it was like light coming in and a weight lifting. He immediately went to tell someone he was accountable to in ministry and submitted to the resultant discipline. He owned what he had done and took responsibility for the wrongdoing. He spoke of the impact of his wrong actions on others and was gutted by the hurt he had caused. His acceptance and repentance were profound and real. It is unlikely that he will ever return to ministry, but he will be able to rebuild his life and find personal restoration.

---

6   In 2 Corinthians 7:10 it says: 'Godly sorrow brings repentance that leads to salvation and leaves no regret, but worldly sorrow brings death.'

It's all over

Even though Saul doesn't die for another sixteen chapters, this was the end of his story as far as Samuel was concerned. He didn't see him again until the day he died, but he continued to mourn for him.

Some theologians believe that Saul was destined to fail, to show the people what a bad idea a king was. Saul was tall, handsome and an impressive warrior – everything they might have hoped for in a king. Yet he failed them. But I don't believe Saul was stitched up by God to fail. When Samuel originally announced the new king Saul, he said that there was a choice: 'If you fear the LORD and serve and obey him and do not rebel against his commands, and if both you and the king who reigns over you follow the LORD your God – good!' (1 Samuel 12:14). God later said to Samuel, 'I regret that I have made Saul king, because he has turned away from me and has not carried out my instructions' (1 Samuel 15:11). When Saul was ultimately rejected, Samuel told him,

'You have not kept the command the LORD your God gave you; *if* you had, he *would have* established your kingdom over Israel for all time. But *now* your kingdom will not endure; the LORD has sought out a man after his own heart and appointed him ruler of his people, *because* you have not kept the LORD's command.'
(1 Samuel 13:13–14, my italics)

Saul's failure lay with his disobedience.

6

David

Looking for a new king

Saul was still king and would be for a while, but God's focus was now on his replacement. This time his choice was completely different. Samuel was sent to anoint the next king (1 Samuel 16:1). Understandably he was a little bit concerned that this wasn't a good political move and could damage his life expectancy. After all, there was still a king, and that king seemed to be getting more paranoid and short-tempered by the day.

God wasn't worried about Saul. God sent Samuel to the family of Jesse in Bethlehem. When Samuel arrived, the elders panicked and asked if they were in trouble. It must have been a bit like when you see a police officer or get told to go to the headteacher (or bishop!).

Samuel met Jesse and his sons. First, he noticed Eliab and just one look convinced him that he was the one God had chosen. God's response to this has become one of the most famous verses in 1 Samuel: 'Do not consider his appearance or his height, for I have rejected him. The LORD does not look at the things people look at. People look at the outward appearance, but the LORD looks at the heart' (1 Samuel 16:7). Samuel should have known this because despite Saul's good looks, inside he was small, weak and desperate to impress people. His spiritual stature was nothing like his physical size. How often people look good outwardly when in fact they are struggling.

Years ago, when preaching on this topic, I came across a story about a young American army officer called John. It all began when he bought a second-hand book and found himself more interested in the pencil notes in the margins than the text of the book itself. From the name written in the front, he was able to locate the address of the book's previous owner, and the author of the notes. He wrote to her and asked if they could correspond, but he was soon deployed as part of the Second World War. For the next year they wrote to each other, and the more they got to know each other, the closer their hearts became. Eventually he requested a photo, but she refused, thinking that looks should be irrelevant to their affection.

When John returned from Europe, they arranged to meet at Grand Central station in New York. She said that she would wear a red rose on her lapel. He scanned the crowd for the woman who had captivated his heart. He noticed a beautiful young lady in a green coat, whom he was instantly drawn to. As she passed, she asked if he was going her way. He made to join her, forgetting the rose. But then he saw it. Directly behind the young lady was an older woman with a red rose. There was nothing of the attractiveness of the lady in the green coat. He felt torn between the physical draw of the young lady and the depth of his longing for the woman who had captured his heart and spirit.

He stepped towards the older woman, gripping the book that had brought them together. Even if he was not physically attracted to her, the friendship would be more profound. As he spoke, he felt the conflict of disappointment and yet affection. He introduced himself and invited her to dinner. The woman broke into a smile and said that she had no idea what was going on, but the young lady in the green coat had begged her to wear this rose. She had said that if he invited her to dinner, she was to say that the young lady was waiting for him in the restaurant across the street and that it was some kind of test![1]

Are we swayed by outward appearance alone or do we look deeper? God is not impressed by looks, wealth or status. Equally,

---

[1] As told in Max Lucado's *And the Angels Were Silent* (Nashville: Thomas Nelson, 2012).

he's not dismissive of the poor, the physically unattractive or the unqualified. He looks at the heart.

Finding the next king

Samuel obediently rejected Eliab and moved on to number two, Abinadab, but God hadn't chosen him either. This process was repeated for all six of the sons Jesse presented. Somewhat confused, Samuel asked him if these were all his sons. It turned out there was another, the youngest. Jesse hadn't even thought of him, since he was just a boy, out looking after the sheep.

They sent for him and as soon as David walked in, Samuel knew that he was the one. He anointed him in front of his whole family. Judging by the next few chapters, they never really got what was going on, but it must have been quite a moment. The Holy Spirit came on David in power, in stark contrast to the following verses, which talk of the Spirit leaving Saul.

David was the least of his family. He was the one who was forgotten and left out. It reminds me of picking teams at school. That moment when not only are you one of the last to be picked, but then the captains argue over who should have to take you. (Or maybe that was just me!) David, the forgotten, was suddenly the chosen one. The reason given throughout Scripture for God's choice is that he was a man after God's heart: 'I have found David son of Jesse, a man after my own heart; he will do everything I want him to do' (Acts 13:22).

An ungodly battle

We get to see David's heart very quickly. Since Saul was distracted by his over-the-top edict on eating food that nearly cost him his son, the Philistines had had the chance to escape and regroup. They became more and more of a problem, resulting in an all-out battle between the two nations, one on either side of a valley, preparing to fight.

As the tension mounted, one of the Philistines, Goliath, stepped forward and lay down a challenge. Instead of a battle, he offered for one of the Israelites to take him on in one-on-one combat. The winner would take it all. Although this was a recognised form of warfare in those days, it was one they didn't need to agree to. It changed the whole focus of the fight. Goliath was enormous – no one could come close to him in terms of size or strength. His armour alone weighed about 57 kg – that's the same weight as Nicole Kidman, according to the internet (although, really, how does the internet know?). His spear had a metal point weighing 7 kg. That's the weight of a Cavalier King Charles spaniel. He was enough to scare the bravest soldier (Goliath, that is, not a Cavalier King Charles spaniel!). So, Goliath was standing before them, goading the Israelites and shouting, 'Why do you come out and line up for battle? Am I not a Philistine, and are you not the servants of Saul?' (1 Samuel 17:8).

Sadly for Goliath, he got it completely wrong. They weren't servants of Saul; they were servants of God. In those days the king tended to be the biggest warrior. As such, he led the charge and was the focus of the people's hope. That had always been the danger with Israel demanding a king; they would place their hope in him rather than God. It was Saul's failing. He felt he had to be the biggest and best rather than simply God's chosen, humble servant. All it took was for a bigger warrior to come along and everything was lost. Goliath's challenge sent Saul and all Israel into terror and despair. Fear made them forget their true identity and source of confidence.

It is good to be inspired by our leaders, by their lives and examples, but they must never eclipse our focus on God. All leaders can and do fail. We need to remember that it is God's church, not the pastor's. In recent times, the abusive behaviour of some

Christian leaders in the UK has been uncovered. One of them is Mike Pilavachi. He started and ran Soul Survivor, probably the most significant youth festival in the UK, with a global impact. It has been difficult for everyone to hear about what was happening behind the scenes at Soul Survivor. One of the most painful aspects for me has been listening to other people questioning all that God did in and through Soul Survivor festivals. It is, of course, good and right that we ask tough questions for our experiences and of Soul Survivor and to discern how we can prevent these things from happening again. And yet, despite all of the pain and the mess, God has moved in so many lives through broken people. It's the same story throughout the Bible, and it's the same story for each of us today. Whilst we may have not done anything as damaging, our brokenness will still impact others in ways that we are often unaware of. And, thank God, he still chooses to use us despite the cracks in our souls.

God is bigger than Goliath

Into this scene of fear and dejection stepped young David. He was sent by his dad, laden with cheese (!) to ingratiate his family with the brothers' commander and check they were OK.[2] He must have been excited. A young lad, getting to visit a real battle. He was going to see God's people striding out against his enemies under God's banner. Imagine his confusion when he was met with men quaking with terror in the camp. Men driven into despair by each other's fear. Thousands of soldiers cowering at the intimidation of one man.

David couldn't understand it and asked loads of people what on

---

2 In case you were wondering, it was ten cheeses for the brothers and ten for the commander. Sadly, we aren't told how big a cheese was, but even twenty mini cheese truckles seems a lot to carry. He also had some bread to go with it – he wasn't mad (1 Samuel 17:17–18).

earth was going on. His big brother put him in his place by saying, 'What are you even doing here, kid? Why have you left your pitiful little flock of sheep to watch grown men at battle?' Oh, the irony. David's response was the cry of younger brothers across history, 'Now what have I done? Can't I even speak?' (see 1 Samuel 17).

Just that one sentence from his brother could have been enough to crush him. He was thrust back into being a child made to feel useless and pathetic by his big brother. There are echoes of Joseph here. He had a choice. He could stay or he could choose to creep away, back to his flocks. This was surely enough to make him doubt himself and feel insignificant. But David knew it wasn't about him or his weakness; this was about God.

The devil is called 'the father of lies' (John 8:44). He lied from the very beginning. The fall in Eden was based on his lies about God. His greatest weapon is the lies he makes us believe about ourselves. The most important thing as a Christian is our identity in Christ. Every Christian is a precious and loved child of God. It is little wonder that the most contested thing in Christian faith is our identity. Most of us question and doubt that God really loves or accepts us. The devil doesn't need to use dramatic means to sow lies that erode our identity and faith. All he needs to do is let us dwell on the voices of others and things that people have said to us over the years.

One of the biggest causes of disease in the world is poor sanitation. When what people excrete stays around, and even ends up in the water supply, it causes untold problems. The most amazing invention is the flush; it takes the unhealthy stuff away. One of the biggest threats to emotional and spiritual health is negative lies. For most of us, compliments and positive words are so easily dismissed or forgotten, whereas negative words get stuck in our minds and fester. We need to flush them away. This is easier said than done, because either the negative lies feel so real or we've stopped recognising them. When someone points them out it can easily become confrontational, or when we spot them we can spiral into condemnation. That's the cue to *flush*.

For a long time at our church, if someone spoke something unhelpful over someone else or we heard someone speaking something over themselves, someone would say 'Flush!' and make the gesture of flushing a toilet (we found the old-fashioned pull-chain flush was the most visually satisfying). This challenges the negative words without sounding harsh or telling someone off. It also breaks the intensity, and normally helps the person spot the lie while smiling. It also works when you're on your own. When you spot yourself spiralling into a negative train of thought, you can say 'Flush!' to yourself and even do the action. This then begins to break the thought pattern.

Last week I came across the following anonymous quote: 'Some people need to be told they are worthy, that they are loved, not because nobody ever told them before, but because someone told them they weren't.' Fortunately David was secure in his identity and in God. He didn't come under the lies. He stayed.

Another day, another predator

Saul heard about David's questioning and summoned him for a royal audience. David simply told him about his experiences as a shepherd. He told the king that when a big bear or a lion came to attack his dad's sheep, God delivered him, and the sheep, safely. He said that this was no different, except that Goliath was just a bit less hairy! He offered to fight him.

You have got to wonder how, in an army of thousands, this lad's curiosity made it back to the king. Perhaps when everyone had given up, someone going against the flow got noticed. Just one person can totally change the atmosphere and attitude of thousands.

In the late nineteenth century, 4,000 young men were being trained by the navy in Plymouth. On their day off they simply wandered the streets. This came to the attention of Agnes Weston, a young woman from Bath. She started a gathering for them, which grew and grew. She then began to provide accommodation for sailors, away from the taverns and brothels. Over time she even secured ways for sailors' pay to go directly to their families rather than being lost in taverns or other activities. Her work became known as Aggie's and to this day provides pastoral support to sailors and their families on UK naval bases. One woman, who started as a Sunday school teacher, was motivated by God to act. Her actions have impacted the lives of thousands of sailors for around 150 years.[3]

The Israelite army saw a scary enemy, but David saw a threat that was no greater than anything he faced in his daily life as a shepherd. God can prepare us through the mundane tasks of life if we allow him.

I will always remember visiting an older man from a church where I used to work. He was the one who asked the dreaded pedantic questions about the church accounts at every annual meeting. Totally unexpectedly, in the middle of the night, his son died. I arrived a few hours later, early the next morning. His son was my age and had left behind a widow. I had no words of wisdom or comfort. I had nothing to offer. In the end, lacking anything else, I suggested that we pray. I prayed falteringly for him. Then he prayed. It was the most profound prayer, and I remember it to this day. It was packed with phrases from the Bible and worship songs of old. This possibly unimpressive old man, in the mundane day to day of life, had filled his soul with wisdom and truth from God. In his moment of devastation and crisis, this is what came to the fore.

---

3 www.aggies.org.uk

Going as himself

Out of options, Saul agreed to let David go to face Goliath. I'm assuming he knew that it was not ideal to send out a boy to get slaughtered. But who knew? David could get lucky. Saul tried to dress David in his own armour, but when he tried it on he could hardly walk, and he had the wisdom to refuse to wear it.

There were two things going on here: David being himself and David knowing who he was representing. Saul wanted David to take on his armour and persona. He wanted it to look as though he was fighting. But David refused to adopt someone else's identity. He was going to be himself.

Similarly, we must not try to be someone else. As I prepared to be interviewed for the role of Bishop of Plymouth, I was given two key bits of advice. First, I would need to prove that I had the appropriate gravitas for such a role. I needed to demonstrate that I was far more than simply someone predominantly focused on young people, with a penchant for making cheeky (and honestly sometimes inappropriate) comments. Second, I would need to demonstrate a breadth of experience and understanding across the Church of England.

The interview began with a five-minute mini-sermon on two passages. I started by retelling the story of the first passage and trying to bring it to life. The second passage could be used to explain the theology of communion, so I attempted to unpack this as well, to demonstrate my profound eucharistic theology. When asked about growing a church, I talked about my work in rural churches. I never mentioned the church we had planted for young people. Throughout the interview, I tried to underline my maturity and seriousness.

I was later given feedback on the interview. I was told that my homily had begun well and was really engaging, but then seemed to dry up and peter out as I talked about the second passage, and that it would have been better just to talk about the first passage. They also commented that they were confused as to why I hadn't talked about the church we had started, to reach young people, when asked about growing a church. Most of all, they said that I seemed to lack my usual *joie de vivre* and sense of fun in the interview and I had been overly serious. It was perceptive and honest. The weaknesses they highlighted were when I wasn't being fully myself and I was trying to impress them. It makes it all the more incredible that I got the job!

In refusing Saul's armour, David also went prophetically as God's representative, not Saul's. David's question to the soldiers in the camp was, 'Who is this uncircumcised Philistine that he should defy the armies of the living God?' (1 Samuel 17:26). He knew they weren't Saul's army.

Goliath was uncircumcised and was missing the physical mark of being one of God's people. Just a side note for those who stumble on the detail or have an overactive imagination: it's not that they were fighting naked. David knew Goliath was uncircumcised, because he wasn't an Israelite, so he wouldn't have been circumcised. David knew without needing to check. That would have been dangerous with a large warrior!

Saul, the donkey herder, was sent by his dad to check on the well-being of his donkeys. David, the shepherd boy, was sent by his dad to check on the well-being of his brothers. Both encountered the unexpected call of God. Saul's focus was on himself and his own shaky ability. David's attention was on God and his unfailing faithfulness and power.

Born to be king

David faced Goliath and, as we all know,[4] with just a few small stones rescued Israel from the Philistines. Saul's initial relief and gratitude quickly dissipated and were replaced with jealousy. If anyone should have been jealous of David it was Saul's son Jonathan.

---

4   If you don't know, you're missing out and need to read 1 Samuel 17.

Jonathan had spent all his life destined to succeed his dad as king. It was the hereditary next step, and Jonathan had all the natural attributes of a king. He was a wise and brave warrior and a good leader of men. However, as soon as he met David, he loved him and saw that David should be king. In fact, he generously gave David his markers of being a prince – his robe, his tunic, his sword, his bow and his belt – as an act of covenant.

Jonathan, therefore, was a remarkable young man. He was full of ambition, vision and passion, yet readily stepped aside for someone else. How many people, and especially leaders, have messed up because they are so desperate to hold on to a position of power rather than step aside? Holy Trinity Brompton is an Anglican church that has probably had a greater effect on the church in England, let alone the Church of England, than any other. I wonder how much of this dates back to a leader of the church at a time when no one had heard of it. In 1985 John Collins, the vicar, discerned that his curate would be better at leading the church than he was. Instead of being threatened by this, he stepped aside so that Sandy Millar, his curate, could take his place.[5]

There is a fascinating book called *Consiglieri* by Richard Hytner.[6] A consiglieri is an advisor or deputy to a mafia boss. The book says that much leadership training focuses on being in charge, when there is as much value in aspiring to the second chair in leadership. This position has huge potential for shaping decisions, managing crises, and strategic development.

Within the Church, the expectation is that church leaders should all want to be the most senior. I know some incredibly gifted and fulfilled clergy who are thriving in the second chair and are keen not to take on ultimate responsibility, yet can feel an external pressure to do so. They feel that their strengths and gifts are

---

5 See: <https://yournameislikehoney.com/2023/05/19/a-life-lived-well>.

6 Richard Hytner, *Consiglieri – Leading from the Shadows* (Profile Books, 2014).

utilised far more where they are. Like Jonathan, they recognise that someone else is better placed to take the lead.

Threatened

Jonathan became David's closest friend. He was willing to risk his life for him. At the same time, Saul became obsessed with jealousy towards David. It wasn't helped by a silly ditty, a song about Saul defeating thousands and David tens of thousands. Saul saw David's success and contrasted it with his own failure. He saw the Lord's presence with David and realised that God's Spirit had left him (1 Samuel 16:14). He began a long, demented journey of bitterness. In outbursts of anger, Saul threw spears at David, but miraculously always missed.

Saul decided he would let the Philistines finish David off for him. So he sent David into more battles. This only added to David's popularity as he achieved more and more military success. Saul offered David a daughter in return for fighting for him, but David humbly turned him down. Then when Saul realised that another daughter, Michal, was keen on David, and he on her, Saul used the daughter as a pawn in his murderous schemes. For David to be allowed to marry Michal, he demanded 100 Philistine foreskins. Eeeugh! David presented him with 200, just to really rub his nose in it (again a strong imagination is unhelpful!).

Saul, rather than appreciating David's successes for Israel, instantly feared for *his* kingdom, forgetting that it wasn't his kingdom in the first place. As leaders, it is easy to think of it as 'our church' or 'our ministry' or 'our group'. If we see the church as ours, we can assume an unhealthy sense of responsibility for it. This can lead to both possessiveness and control.

In the early years of Unlimited, as a small church it made a huge difference whether or not individuals attended. There was one lad who was one of the first people to find faith with us. When he turned up, you knew he was there. But he wasn't the most reliable. He was also a natural leader, but his faith didn't fully impact the way he lived life. He was someone we deeply cared for and wanted to see flourish in his faith and life. I would therefore get so frustrated when he said he was coming and then didn't show up, or when his behaviour was inappropriate. I put it down to my concern for his discipleship and would try to gently, and even not so gently, challenge him. Our mission statement as a church was to help 'young people to encounter the God they'd never met and to live the difference'. Subconsciously, his faith journey had become a marker to me as to how much we were living out our mission. I began to recognise that I perceived the 'success' of the church as being dependent on my leadership. I had made it my church.

When we see it as 'our church', we put reliance on our leadership rather than on God. At the same time any failure in the church, or of the church, becomes our failure. Any criticism of the church becomes criticism of us. Any issues around power quickly get personal, just as they did for Saul. There is no longer space for risk and space for others to develop and flourish in their gifts and leadership.

Signs and circumstances

The rest of Saul's life was given over to trying to take David's. In the process, David became an outlaw, living in caves with some of the lowlifes of the day. David had the opportunity to kill Saul. People urged him to. Once, David and his men were hiding in the back of a cave (1 Samuel 24) when Saul chose the very same cave in which to relieve himself. But despite Saul being completely unguarded and alone, David resisted. His men believed that this was God handing Saul over to David.

David was wise enough to recognise that this 'sign' would contradict God's word. He knew that it was forbidden to strike down God's chosen one. This is a helpful reminder to us all. We shouldn't assume an apparent 'sign' is a message from God. You probably know that when someone in your family is pregnant, you can suddenly see pregnant women everywhere. Or when you buy a blue car, suddenly you see more blue cars. But this is a reflection of our heightened awareness, not an increase in pregnancies or blue cars! Similarly, when we ask God for a sign, we are more alert to seeing the sign we're hoping for. Any perceived sign needs to be weighed alongside Scripture and also common sense. Remember – God doesn't contradict himself.

David had learned to trust God, fight and worship on the hills whilst a shepherd, and in this situation he grew in leadership and character. Many times he faced death, but he kept trusting and obeying God. I meet many people who say they will focus on their faith when life gets back on track. David shows us that we can meet God anywhere, in any circumstances. In fact, engaging with God and his call on our lives in the tough times is the best way to get back on track. There's a danger that 'one day' will never come. There is always a reason not to prioritise God. Life is always complicated. But as Jesus said, we must seek first the kingdom of God and everything else will follow (Matthew 6:33).

Sorrow versus godly sorrow

David was resolute: he couldn't lay a finger on the Lord's anointed. As we know, God had removed his anointing from Saul, but it was still not David's place to take him down. That right belonged to God alone. As Saul left the cave, David called out to him, telling him all that had happened. Saul was overcome with emotion and wept, but he didn't change at a deeper level. His attitude and actions were the same and he continued to hunt David down.

On one occasion David and one of his men went into the middle of Saul's camp while they were asleep (1 Samuel 26). They stood over Saul as he slept. Again, David's man told him that God had given Saul into his hands. But David stood firm, merely taking Saul's water jug and spear. From a safe distance David called out to Saul, and again Saul was deeply moved that David spared his life. This time he confessed that he had sinned by pursuing David and invited him back into the fold.

We can be deeply distressed by the effects of habitual sin in our lives. Outwardly we may want to change, but it needs to be deeper than that. Saul's insecurity and jealousy had taken over. For him, murder was an acceptable cost. He was sorry, but not willing to change and root out the real issues behind his obsessive fixation on David. Real repentance was needed to make a difference, rather than a bit of regret. As Paul says, 'Godly sorrow brings repentance that leads to salvation and leaves no regret' (2 Corinthians 7:10). Godly sorrow, rather than being stuck in regret, leads to deep repentance, with the recognition and open owning of the roots of the failure.

Conclusion

At the end of Saul's journey, his insecurities continued to manifest. His obsession with David got so bad that he started to consult with the dead when God stopped talking to him. This was a significant marker of his turning from God (1 Samuel 28). Eventually, Saul and his son Jonathan died in battle with the Philistines, which is ironic because he should have wiped them out years earlier (1 Samuel 14). Saul could have succeeded as king, but instead was unfaithful to God and his reign fell apart (1 Chronicles 10:13). What a sad tale to have been chosen as the first king of Israel and then spend most of your reign trying to prevent someone else being chosen and taking your place.

The king is dead – long live the king

David had waited since his youth to become King of Israel. God called him from the obscurity of a hillside to the palace. He alone had the faith to defeat Goliath. He had become a great leader in God's army and even married the king's daughter. He had known his destiny before even meeting Saul, but the journey to the throne couldn't have been harder. It meant abandoning his family, living in caves, constantly fearing for his life and being hunted down like an animal. Therefore, you would expect that when Saul died, David would have been leading the celebrations. Instead, he was grief stricken. He sang a song of lament for both Saul and Jonathan, noting their great worth and achievements (2 Samuel 1).

Earlier we saw Samuel's grief over God's declaration that Saul's reign was over, but David's reaction to Saul's death was even more poignant. It took something special to be able to see the best in a man who was obsessed with your death. What a challenge to work to find good in all people. We can't be responsible for how others treat us, but we are responsible for how we react.

Years ago, when I was a parish priest, there was a confrontation between two people in the village. It was just one incident of many between them over the years. This time, I got caught in the middle as I intervened and called the police. Later that evening, I went to visit one of the men to make sure he was OK. He refused to speak to me. I did all I could to resolve things, but to no avail.

A week later, I was walking through the village and he made a show of pretending to drive his car at me. A few days later, when I took my children to the village primary school, I found myself walking down the corridor towards the very same man. He looked up, saw me and turned on his heel and walked away. This became a daily routine.

At first it annoyed me. Then it became a bit of a game. How far down the corridor could I get before he noticed me? If I timed it right, would he go into the cupboard to avoid me? After a few days, I realised my attitude might not be the most appropriate or godly. And so, each day when I saw him, I began to use it as a prompt to pray for him.

Someone else's behaviour shouldn't determine ours. Just because he treated me badly didn't mean I should reciprocate. As Jesus said, 'Love your enemies and pray for those who persecute you' (Matthew 5:44). No one is beyond God's love and compassion, and we need to demonstrate that love and compassion too.

Dealing with the fallout

It took a long time for David to work through the mess Saul had left behind in Israel. There would be many battles and struggles between the houses of David and Saul (2 Samuel 2–4). There was intrigue, subterfuge and people changing sides for personal gain. Eventually, David became king (2 Samuel 5:1–4) and he began to put things in order.

First, he dealt with the Philistines. In contrast with Saul, he sought God's revelation and wisdom to do this. He didn't just ask God's permission, but continued to seek his guidance in the details. God's instructions were wonderfully comprehensive:

'Do not go straight up, but circle round behind them and attack them in front of the poplar trees. As soon as you hear the sound of marching in the tops of the poplar trees, move quickly, because that will mean the LORD has gone out in front of you to strike the Philistine army.' So David did as the LORD commanded him.
(2 Samuel 5:23–25)

When Saul consulted God, it was more as a religious or superstitious practice. But David constantly sought God's direction, not just when he was desperate. What a great model for us as Christians. I've always been intrigued by churches that have signs outside giving the service times followed by 'DV' – an abbreviation for the Latin *Deo volente*, meaning 'God willing'. Do they actively check before each service whether it is God's will, or do they assume it must be, provided the church isn't falling down? If the preacher is ill, do they take that as a sign that God is not willing, or do they find a replacement?

We want to live according to God's guidance, but if we're honest, we make our plans and hope God will intervene if necessary. Seeking God's guidance can be really tough. If we have a sense of God speaking or acting, we always need to weigh and discern this with others and against Scripture. We need to hold it lightly and not claim that God has categorically spoken. We need to be ready to admit that we might have misheard or misunderstood.

Yet if our loving heavenly Father, the God of the universe, has wisdom and guidance for us, we need to be led by it, even if we will get it wrong sometimes. I am always hugely encouraged that Jesus likened us to sheep recognising their master's voice (John 10:1ff.). If even sheep are able to identify their shepherd's voice, there must be hope for us!

God at the heart of the community

Once he had dealt with the Philistines, David called the people together, because he'd decided it was time for the ark to return to the people of Israel. Not Noah's, that was long gone, but the ark of the covenant. This was symbolic of God being with them, the place where he caused his presence to dwell on earth. Nothing was more precious, valuable or significant than the ark to the identity of the Israelites.

Somehow over time the Israelites had begun to lose their sense of awe for the ark. It had become more of a mascot than God's holy presence. When Samuel was young, there was a battle against the Philistines that went disastrously wrong (1 Samuel 4:1ff.) and 4,000 men were killed. Someone had the genius idea to grab the ark and take that into battle to protect them. It had been relegated to the role of a lucky talisman.

When the ark arrived in Israel's camp at the battlefield, the Israelites roared so loudly that the Philistines heard. The Philistines recognised that a god was in the camp. They also knew it was the same God who had defeated the Egyptians. But rather than this demoralising them, or causing them to give in, instead it rallied them to fight harder. That day they killed 30,000 men and captured the ark.

Eli, the chief priest of Israel (and incidentally the guy who brought up Samuel), heard the news and died from the shock. Well, technically he died from being obese and falling off his chair in shock and breaking his neck (1 Samuel 4:18). The same day his daughter-in-law gave birth and called the son Ichabod, meaning 'no glory', because the glory had departed from Israel. Such was the immense significance of losing the ark.

The Philistines put the captured ark, their battle spoil, in the temple of Dagon (one of their gods) in the city of Ashdod. The first night, when no one was around, the statue of Dagon fell prostrate before the ark. They propped it back up, but the next night it fell again and this time its hands and head fell off. Then the Philistines began to get tumours. It was all too much for the people of Ashdod and they tried to send the ark away, but no one else wanted it. Everyone was too scared. They could see that when people housed it, inhabitants started dying.

After seven months the Philistines couldn't stand it any longer and they sent the ark back to Israel on a cart, with golden gifts beside it. No one wanted to be anywhere near it, so they let cows pull the cart and left the route to chance. The cows wandered to Beth Shemesh, an Israelite village nineteen miles from Jerusalem.

There, when it arrived, seventy men couldn't overcome their curiosity, so casually had a sneaky peek inside. They all died (1 Samuel 6:19). People from the village began to ask, 'Who can stand in the presence of the LORD, this holy God?' (verse 20). At last they were beginning to get it! But they still responded in fear. Rather than repenting and endeavouring to restore it to its rightful place in Jerusalem with the king, they asked the people of Kiriath Jearim, a village ten miles from Jerusalem, to look after it for them, which they did. It stayed there for all of Saul's reign. The presence of God, tucked to the side, much like in Saul's heart.

It's so sad when people get so close to understanding and then completely miss the point. The ark was brought into battle as a mascot. The enemy understood its significance and yet the Israelites, in their familiarity, didn't. The Philistines saw the consuming might of God's holiness and sent it away after only a few months. The Israelites who received it back casually looked inside and only then recognised God's holy presence.

It is so easy to take God and his love and forgiveness for granted. We can be chummy with him and miss the awe and reverence. But the other danger is that we recognise something of God's awesomeness and holiness and are then too fearful to relate to him.

Many people understand God to be so transcendent and awesome that he is distant and not relevant in our day-to-day lives. Others see him as so immanent, or intimate, that they are too familiar with him, without any sense of awe or reverence. I find it offensive when people say to me (and they have) that modern worship treats Jesus as our boyfriend. But there is a real danger that our worship can make our feelings the focus.

Intimacy is a vital aspect of worship, as the charismatic stream of the Church has helped us discover, but it needs to be held alongside awe and holiness. It needs to focus on God, not us. The challenge of faith, and for our relationship with God, is to hold both the immanence and transcendence in balance. They are both utterly true. It is worth reflecting on how we view God and how that influences our attitude and behaviour towards him.

Our attitude to God

David knew that it was of primary importance to get the ark back (2 Samuel 6). He knew that they needed God's presence at the heart of his kingdom. So David built a cart like the one the Philistines used, only snazzier (2 Samuel 6:3ff.). The Israelites loaded up the cart with the ark and began to celebrate and worship as they brought it home to Jerusalem. During the journey, one of the oxen lost its footing. Uzzah (one of the people accompanying the ark on its journey home) grabbed at the ark and was instantly killed by God for his irreverent act.

This may seem slightly harsh. We could argue that poor Uzzah was simply trying to protect the ark. But the reality is that he wouldn't have been strong enough to save it if it was actually falling. Furthermore, his presumption to touch it defied all God's instructions for the ark. In that one action, Uzzah presumed that he could rescue God.

At the time, David didn't understand God's actions. He couldn't understand why Uzzah had to die. He got angry and a bit afraid. He cried out, 'How can the ark of the LORD ever come to me?' (2 Samuel 6:9). But this statement is revealing. The whole journey was meant to be about God returning to his rightful place. It was not meant to be about the ark coming to David. His cries show us that he thought getting the ark back to the heart of Israel was also about him.

We all have mixed motives. In Jeremiah it says, 'The heart is deceitful above all things and beyond cure. Who can understand it?' (Jeremiah 17:9). Only God truly knows what's going on inside us. It's easy for us to go one of two ways: to come under huge guilt and self-condemnation, or to dismiss any sense that our motives might be anything other than entirely pure. We need to avoid both extremes.

When we, or others, discern that our attitude may be wrong, we don't need to come under shame or condemnation, but we do need to own it and repent of it. It is important that we don't take the credit or attention that belongs to God and make it all about us. We shouldn't be doing things to make ourselves look good or increase our status. But equally we have a part to play and are called to partner with God, and like John the Baptist our lives are called to point to Jesus.

It's all about God

Following the death of Uzzah, in his fear and distress, David gave up on his mission to move the ark and left it at Obed-Edom's house. For the next three months Obed-Edom was seriously blessed and David heard about it. After much prayer and reflection, he made another attempt to return the ark. This time the ark recovery was done properly. Clearly David had been swotting up. He instructed the people that the ark must be carried on poles rather than on a cart, and only by Levites (1 Chronicles 15). Every six steps he sacrificed a bull and fattened calf. This was far more dignified than the rickety cow cart. The ark was carried in a position of honour, with the priests feeling the full weight of its glory. They knew that God was with them and helping them. Sacrifices were offered out of awe and gratitude to God. What a contrast!

As all this was happening, David danced with the procession and worshipped God with all his might. There was no space for the focus to be on him, unlike before. It was a spectacular celebration, and everyone was rejoicing. Well, everyone except David's wife, Michal. When David came within sight of the palace Michal was appalled. She could only see shame in his being stripped down to his undergarment of a linen ephod and dancing in unrestrained worship.[7]

---

7   A linen ephod was actually a priestly garment. David stripped off his royal robes. At the coronation of King Charles III, something of this symbolism was echoed in his anointing.

David didn't care how undignified or humiliated he was before God. This moment, this celebration, was not about him and how he appeared, but was all about God. That is something I need to take hold of daily. I need to discern whether I am more concerned about how I appear to others or if I am living for the audience of one – God.

This challenge is particularly illustrated in corporate worship. We need to ask ourselves: 'Is my sung worship about me and for my satisfaction, or is it all about God?' If we're honest, so much of people's attitude to church on a Sunday is focused on whether they like the service and what they want out of it. Sunday worship is so easily about us rather than God.

Mishearing God

Once the ark was back at the heart of Israel in Jerusalem, David settled into his palace and enjoyed a bit of peace from his enemies. He sent for the prophet Nathan and said that it wasn't OK for him to be in a palace while the ark was in a tent (1 Chronicles 17). David wanted to build a temple for the Lord. Nathan's spontaneous reaction was to tell David that he should do whatever it was he had in mind, because God was with him. However, that night God told Nathan that David's mind was not aligned with his at all. God also gave Nathan a full recap of David's life story so far and made huge promises for David's future family. But at the same time he said that he couldn't build the temple (2 Samuel 7:5–16).

Two things stand out from this: first, just because we have God with us doesn't mean we can't get it wrong. Various great Christian leaders who are clearly gifted through God end up going astray. I recently met a seemingly lovely pastoral leader. He was deeply concerned for those in his care. But it soon became apparent he believed that God was leading him into deeply inappropriate behaviour. He had begun to dominate those in his care. He was convinced that he knew what was wrong in other people's lives and so manipulated them, however unknowingly, around his perceptions. He was utterly convinced that God was with him, and that he was hearing God unfalteringly. This resulted in him crossing into spiritual abuse.

There is a very real danger, with Christian celebrity culture and podcasts, that people will follow the teaching of a preacher without question. We have no concept of the character, maturity or actual leadership of a person we just listen to online. We can't see the outworking of their faith in their own context. Nobody has perfect theology or understanding. We all have our weaknesses and misunderstandings of God's word. Even Nathan the prophet made a wrong assumption. He assumed that if David desired something it must be in line with God's will.

The second point to note is that God loved David and was completely on his side, but that didn't mean David got his own way. God not agreeing with David's temple wasn't a rejection. It is so easy for us to feel rejected when God doesn't choose us to do something we want to do for him. But that is not the reality. God's will really is good, pleasing and perfect. It just rarely completely aligns with ours (1 Chronicles 21)!

The senseless census

As he settled into the role of king, David decided that it would be a good idea to take a census.[8] This was not a good idea and had terrible consequences. It says in 1 Chronicles 21:1 that Satan incited David to take the census. In 2 Samuel 24:1, it says that in his anger against Israel, because of their waywardness, God incited David.

The accounts, at first glance, appear to contradict each other. So we'll need to dig a little deeper. If it was God inciting David, then

---

8 Since Samuel was written in topical rather than chronological order, it's not clear when this happened. It is recorded in 2 Samuel 24 and 1 Chronicles 21.

this makes little sense. In this case, David would have been being obedient rather than doing wrong. Also, if God incited David to do wrong, then God was causing him to sin, which goes against his nature. People have argued that the idea 'God incited David' is simply a conflation of the idea of God's sovereignty. If Satan was responsible, he was only able to incite under God's permissive will. In this understanding, 'God was angry, Satan was allowed to provoke David' gets abbreviated to 'God provoked'.

This fits with the fact that, in the epistle of James, it is clear that God does not provoke us to do evil.[9] So God could not have provoked David to evil. Whether you accept this understanding or not, it is important to talk about it, because we shouldn't simply ignore difficult bits in Scripture. At the same time, it is OK not to fully understand something and keep an open mind.

What really matters is that David did something that God had forbidden. Satan was in some way involved, but it's not clear how. This is a challenge for us all; we can be walking with God and still be led astray and there can be a spiritual battle involved. For whatever reason, we can convince ourselves that it's OK to do something God expressly told us not to do. David seems to have convinced himself that it would glorify God to know how big Israel was. But however he justified it, it soon became clear that he had gravely disobeyed God.

As soon as David told Joab, his commander, to get counting, we see that it was wrong. The Israelites were only allowed to count what belonged to them, not what belonged to God. This was presumably to keep their focus on God and his provision and possession of them. Israel didn't belong to David.

When God did command a census, as in Exodus 30:11–12, each person had to pay a ransom, probably as a reminder that they relied on God for their life and it was not their own. In Exodus 30 it says,

---

9 James 1:13 says: 'When tempted, no one should say, "God is tempting me." For God cannot be tempted by evil, nor does he tempt anyone.'

'When you take a census of the Israelites to count them, each one must pay the LORD a ransom for his life at the time he is counted. Then no plague will come on them when you number them.' The importance of numbering people as belonging to God is underlined by one of the possible punishments that arose from David's census. The morning after the census, God sent Gad the prophet to David. He offered David three options: three years of famine, three months of fleeing from enemies or three days of plague.

David said that he would rather be punished by God, whose mercy was great, than fall into the hands of men. This led to a plague sweeping through Israel, which God, in his grief, called to an end. In the wake of the plague, David recognised the consequences of his mistake and was devastated. He cried out that the people were sheep and the sin was his, not theirs.

God commanded him to build an altar on the threshing floor of the farm of Araunah the Jebusite. Understandably Araunah was pretty shocked when King David and an angel turned up. He offered the land for free, but David refused to take it and insisted on paying.[10] David said he would not make a sacrifice that cost him nothing. How easy it is for us to want cheap grace. We know that God will forgive us, so we ignore the effect our wrongdoing has on others and presume upon God's easy forgiveness.

During the Reformation, Martin Luther argued against the corruption that was the Roman Catholic tradition of penance, claiming that they had gone too far in demanding the payment of penance for sins. He was captivated by God's grace, which was freely available to everyone. But as we become confident in that grace, we must make sure we don't neglect real and deep repentance.

---

10 Fun fact: the farm that David bought from Araunah later became the site of the Temple (2 Chronicles 3:1). David wasn't allowed to build it, but he was allowed to start the preparations.

Idle hands and late-night temptation

Life in Israel settled down and became more peaceful. The Israelite army was powerful and David's position as king was secure. All should have been well, but the sense of ease and security was the prelude to spiritual and moral failure. Pride can absolutely come before a fall, but often it's just complacency that trips us up. At the start of 2 Samuel 11, it says, 'In the spring, at the time when kings go off to war, David sent Joab out with the king's men and the whole Israelite army... But David remained in Jerusalem' (verse 1). At the time when kings went to war, David didn't. Uh oh!

The next thing we know, he was up late one night and caught a glimpse of a woman bathing naked. The woman was probably performing a ritual bathing, commanded by the law. She was faithfully following God's instructions. In the days before the internet, David found himself idly looking at naked women late at night.

We don't know if David went up on the roof of the palace in order to see the women bathe, or if it was a coincidence. I'm guessing it was a natural walkway on the palace roof rather than him having to scramble up there to look. But however innocently he caught a first glimpse, he didn't turn away and deny himself a second.

Paul wrote that God 'is faithful; he will not let you be tempted beyond what you can bear. But when you are tempted, he will also provide a way out so that you can endure it' (1 Corinthians 10:13). The problem is, the way out is also the way in. When we are tempted, we need to resist in the first moments rather than assume there will be other escape routes later.

A few years ago, I heard a great youth talk on temptation. The speaker memorably advised the youth to 'flee, not fondle'! It was a great answer to the age-old sex question young people always ask: 'How far can I go before I have to stop?' But, as this speaker recognised, they are asking the wrong question. The only way out of temptation is to flee instantly, not see how close you can get to the line before trying to stop. You don't see how much of a lion you can touch before you worry about it attacking you. This applies to any form of temptation that you are flirting with – not just relationships.

Taking it further

When David saw a very beautiful woman who happened to be naked, he didn't run away. He was intrigued. He wanted to know more. He asked his servants who she was and found out that she was Bathsheba, the wife of Uriah the Hittite. David knew that Uriah was away fighting for Israel, where he should also have been. He had her fetched to the palace.

Who knows how David justified the invitation to himself to ease his conscience. He possibly never intended anything more to happen. But as God warned Cain, 'sin is crouching at your door; it desires to have you, but you must rule over it' (Genesis 4:7). David had fully opened the door. He had sex with her. You might want to question her morality, but David was the king; he had the power and position. He was fully responsible. It didn't matter if she was flattered or interested or neither of those things – she would have had no choice in what happened. She was a victim and he was totally culpable. We need to recognise the responsibility of power and position.

Someone recently did a masters dissertation looking at the power of bishops. In interviews, most bishops first of all spoke of their lack of power, because they are constantly in situations where they are limited in their ability to make necessary change. They have less 'hard power' to change things than people assume. But bishops do have a lot of 'soft power', where they are in spiritual authority over others. This may mean that, in a conversation, someone may be unable to say how they really feel, whether the bishop realises it or not.

In my early days as a bishop, there was one week when three times people referred to things I'd apparently said, none of which were true. In at least two situations, I'd been asking questions without any particular agenda or view, and it had been received as an expression of my opinion. If I ponder out loud it can be seen as my viewpoint, which people then feel they have to act on. However much I want to enable and empower others, I need to own the power I have and be alert to its effect. It is incredibly hard to stand up to someone who has a position of power or authority over us. Even with the most approachable boss or leader in the world, there is still an imbalance of power and freedom of choice. It's hard for people to say no, and saying nothing doesn't mean that people agree. Acquiescence is not the same as consent.

The consequences

The text tells us that Bathsheba had been ritually purifying herself from uncleanness (2 Samuel 11:4). In other words, she'd just had her period. You might think this is too much information, and something we didn't need or want to know, but it meant that when she discovered she was pregnant, there was no doubt who the father was. A fact that David desperately wanted to cover up, so David invited Uriah back from battle, pretending to want an update from the frontline. After hearing a brief report, David 'kindly' suggested that Uriah pop home and 'wash his feet', wink, wink, nudge, nudge!

Disappointingly for David, Uriah was a man of character. He slept with his servants at the entrance to the palace rather than returning home. David incredulously asked him why he didn't go in, and he replied that he couldn't sleep in comfort when the ark and people were encamped on a battleground. Ouch. David not only hadn't bothered going to war, but he had drawn an honourable man's wife into bed while he was away.

Instead of being convicted by this damning contrast with Uriah, David continued to attempt to cover up his sin. He invited Uriah for dinner again, and this time got him drunk in an attempt to loosen his resolve and get him to return to his wife. When this failed, David sent Uriah back to the front and instructed Joab to leave him in an exposed position in battle to get him killed. Uriah died. As soon as a period of mourning had passed, David moved in on the grieving widow, adding her to his collection of wives.

In this tragic unfolding of events, David broke four of the Ten Commandments. He coveted his neighbour's wife, committed adultery, lied and then committed murder. He also forced a woman to have sex with him. How far he fell. This probably all happened while he was still leading amazing worship. There is no sense in Scripture that his faith or spiritual practices had in any way diminished at this time.

None of us are immune to temptation. As we see with David, power and a lack of accountability make our ability to do wrong even more dangerous. We can be passionate worshippers, leading others in their faith and at the same time committing all kinds of sin. Like David, we can blind ourselves to our wrongdoing. We can suppress our conscience to the point that we no longer realise we're in the wrong. So many people who have affairs somehow convince themselves God is OK with it or that it's not their fault.

For David, reality only hit when the prophet Nathan told him an emotional story that went like this: Once upon a time, there was a poor man with only one lamb. And this lamb was more of a member of the family than livestock. His rich neighbour, with all manner of flocks of his own, had a visitor who needed feeding. Rather than killing one of his many animals, he took the poor man's beloved only lamb.

David was outraged by this tale and demanded justice, only for Nathan to tell him that he was that man. He was devastated.

He wasn't just concerned for his reputation or ashamed; he was deeply convicted and repentant.[11] There was nothing he could do to make amends or earn forgiveness. Yet God offered him undeserved mercy. He does the same for us.

David learned that there would still be consequences from his sin. David's actions would inspire the contempt of his enemies, and the baby Bathsheba was carrying would die (2 Samuel 12:13–14). There would also be a lasting effect on his family from his sinfulness. But, due to God's redeeming character, the next child David had with Bathsheba would become the next great king of Israel, King Solomon.

Since becoming a bishop, I have been shocked in a more profound way than ever before by the way some people talk about forgiveness. Sometimes people speak of someone as being totally beyond forgiveness. Others have said to me it is a case of safeguarding gone mad and that people convicted of even the worst offences need to be forgiven. I truly believe that no one is beyond God's forgiveness, but forgiveness does not negate the consequences of sin. We can all experience God's forgiveness, but our actions may have a lasting and even permanent effect on what we can and cannot do in the future. Forgiveness doesn't mean that people are allowed to go back into situations where others can be hurt or put at risk.

We will never know why David fell so catastrophically with Bathsheba. I have a suspicion that he laid the ground for it over time. David had multiple wives. By 2 Samuel 3, he had married Michal, Ahinoam, Abigail, Maakah, Haggith, Abital and Eglah – and they are just the ones we know of! He also had numerous concubines. Polygamy may well have been the norm in those days, especially for kings, but not for God's kings. God had said

---

11 Traditionally, Psalm 51 is seen as David's confession, and modern Bible translations often have a heading attributing it as such. But I haven't ascribed it to him in this paragraph, because there is still some debate among Old Testament scholars.

the king must not have multiple wives, or his heart would be led astray (Deuteronomy 17:17). This is exactly what happened with David.

Tragically, the same happened with his children. As I have said before, just as we inherit qualities from our parents through genetics, we can also inherit from them spiritually. Just after this whole incident we read of David's son Amnon raping his step-sister Tamar (2 Samuel 13). Solomon would be granted all wisdom by God, but he would still be led astray because he took many wives (1 Kings 11:4).

The legacy of David's weakness with women is huge. But God's power is greater than the power of sin. There is much more that could be said of David, his incredible example and failures, but I will end with one last story from his life.

Conclusion: David, a man after God's heart

When David was 'old and well advanced in years' he could no longer keep warm. His servants decided that the best thing would be to find a young virgin to keep him from getting cold. There may not have been electric blankets back then, but surely there must have been other options! And they didn't grab just any virgin. Instead they conducted a thorough search for the most beautiful virgin. You couldn't make this up!

Eventually they found Abishag. Apparently, she 'was very beautiful; she took care of the king and waited on him, but the king had no sexual relations with her' (1 Kings 1:4). David, the one who almost blew it all for sex with a woman, had a gorgeous woman acting as his hot water bottle and he didn't touch her.

Up until very recently I loved this ending to the account of David's life, because I've always seen it as an incredible testimony to God's ability to transform us even in our areas of greatest weakness. It's the wonderful positive ending that I want. But I think I was wrong.[12] I've recognised that I still want things to be neat and tidy. For people to be good or bad. But life is not that simple. It is more likely that in his infirmity David simply wasn't up to it any more. In addition, Abishag's beauty speaks instead more of the pervasive objectification of women – that only the most beautiful woman would do for the king – than David's ability to resist temptation.

As we saw with Goliath, David was someone who consistently saw things from a faith, or God, perspective, when others had a solely human view. The Psalms and accounts of his life show that he was devoted to the law and God's word. He consistently sought to discern God's will, even if he didn't always get it right. He was a man of worship. Whether he wrote lots of the psalms or fewer than we popularly imagine, his life was shaped by an intimate, honest relationship with God. He held nothing back.

Yet this didn't protect him from getting it wrong. In fact, he could be totally blind to his sin, only accepting it when Nathan called him out. As soon as he became aware of his wrongdoing, he did repent, but this didn't reduce the consequences of his sin for himself and all around him.

The Old Testament points to one coming from the line of David who will rescue God's people, so it's easy to focus on how good David was and that he was a man after God's own heart,[13] yet the reality is that even David couldn't lead and save God's people without messing up. God didn't cancel him, but didn't ignore his sin either. Scripture can handle paradox, which we find so hard to hold. David's life and reign show that a king was never going to rescue God's people. In looking to the Son of David, it is not so

---

12 Danielle Strickland's 'Right Side Up' podcast series on clergy abuse has profoundly challenged my understanding, especially Episode 4: 'David – the Patron Saint of Abusive Clergy'. The Church owes Danielle a huge debt for her tireless efforts, at great personal cost, to expose and stand against abuse in the Church.

13 Acts 13:22 says: 'After removing Saul, he made David their king. He testified concerning him: "I have found David son of Jesse, a man after my own heart; he will do everything I want him to do."'

much looking to one like David, but also to one completely unlike him. Not a king or merely human leader, but God himself, made flesh. The Son of David. The Son of Man. The Son of God. The only one who can truly save and lead us.

Part 4

TWELVE GOOD MEN

7

The disciples

Introduction

Many people followed Jesus and became his disciples, but there were twelve men whom he called to be his closest followers: the apostles.

Over the years I've been on numerous interview panels assessing candidates for various positions within churches, schools and charities. In one sense, I love interviewing people. You get to probe and ask all sorts of questions you can't normally ask. It satisfies my immense curiosity (or nosiness) about people. At the same time, I find it really hard, since so much rests on this one moment, both for the applicants and the organisation. Are you actually getting to see the real person and how they would perform in the role? I wonder how much I am being prejudiced by my own perceptions or just gut feelings.

A key piece of advice I was once given is that it is always better not to appoint than to take on the wrong person. This is so true. I've seen the effects of that first-hand on too many occasions. I know several churches that bear the scars of having appointed the wrong leader.

If there was one person who always knew who to appoint, it would be Jesus. He brought none of his own weaknesses, prejudices and failings to the process. He understood people completely and had an untainted ability to hear his Father's revelation and will. Even so, he still took a whole night in prayer and contemplation with his Father before choosing the twelve men who would form his core team. We can fairly assume, therefore, that we are about to be introduced to the finest selection of men in history...

When morning came, he called his disciples to him and chose twelve of them, whom he also designated apostles: Simon (whom he named Peter), his brother Andrew, James, John, Philip, Bartholomew, Matthew, Thomas, James son of Alphaeus, Simon who was called the Zealot, Judas son of James, and Judas Iscariot, who became a traitor.
(Luke 6:13-16)[1]

Andrew

Matthew's Gospel also lists the apostles, starting with 'Simon (who is called Peter)' (Matthew 10:2). Interestingly, Simon may have been listed first because he became the ultimate leader, but he wasn't the first to follow Jesus. That was Andrew. Even so, three of the four gospels don't even bother telling you the back story of Andrew. He just enters the scene with his brother Simon as follows: 'Jesus was walking beside the Sea of Galilee, he saw two brothers, Simon called Peter and his brother Andrew' (Matthew 4:18). Luke doesn't even give him a name check, until he lists him among the twelve apostles, even though he must have been with Simon Peter for the miraculous catch of fish (Luke 5:1ff.).

It is only the Gospel of John that gives us his origin story (John 1:35–42). Prior to both those incidents Andrew had spent at least a day with Jesus. On that day, John the Baptist pointed out Jesus to two of his disciples, calling him the Lamb of God. Those two disciples were intrigued and began to follow Jesus. When Jesus became aware that two blokes were following along behind him, he stopped and asked them what they wanted. A bit thrown, they blurted out the first thing that came into their heads and asked

---

1 As you will see in the coming pages, Jesus called his disciples in different ways, as individuals or in pairs. He chose the twelve apostles from among those who had begun to follow him over a period of time.

him where he was staying. What a bizarre question![2] Jesus very graciously invited them to come and visit his digs. I'm not sure how long it would have taken to have a good look around, but presumably not that long.

However, a quick visit to his lodgings turned into a whole day hanging out with Jesus. I wonder what they did in that day. It's a bit like when Jesus went for dinner with Zacchaeus. I would love to know exactly what they talked about that brought such a transformation.[3] By four in the afternoon, one of them had sussed out who Jesus was (John 1:39–41). That person was Andrew. We have no idea who the other guy was, but Andrew immediately rushed off to find his brother Simon. He told him, '"We have found the Messiah" (that is, the Christ)', and then took him to meet Jesus.

It's so easy to read this account and not think about the enormity of it. Having just spent a day with Jesus, Andrew realised that he was the Messiah. It takes half the gospel for Simon to get it, and when he did, his declaration of faith was a massive moment in the story. In Matthew's Gospel, Jesus even went as far as to say that there was no way Simon could have worked this out for himself. God must have helped him to get there (Matthew 16:17). From the moment Simon understood who Jesus was, the whole focus of the gospel shifted to Jesus' journey to Jerusalem and the cross.

But Andrew clicked immediately and got absolutely no recognition for doing so. In fact, Andrew's instant reaction was to grab his brother and bring him to Jesus. He was the first follower of Jesus and the first evangelist. Surely he was destined for true greatness!

---

2 In fact, there aren't bizarre questions in John; everything has layers of meaning. Without realising it, they are asking God incarnate where he's staying, just as he's made his dwelling on earth. Only twenty-five verses earlier, John wrote, 'The Word became flesh and blood, and moved into the neighborhood' (John 1:14, The Message). This is about so much more than Jesus' Airbnb.

3 If you haven't heard what happened with Zacchaeus, you can find it in Luke 19:1–10. It's one of my favourite interactions from Jesus' life and not just because he was short.

Well, maybe he was, but we don't get to hear about it. As soon as Simon was brought to Jesus, Andrew faded into the background. In fact, of the twelve times Andrew's name occurs in the gospels, six of them specify that he is Simon's brother.

Anyone with a sibling will have sympathy for Andrew. Throughout life, my sister and I have met people who then ask if we are the other's brother or sister. I met a young person a while ago whom I hadn't seen for five years. Given the length of time, I didn't recognise her. When she said her name, my unthinking response was, 'Of course – you're Dan's sister!' A fantastic lad we know has gone through school as 'Smith No. 4', because he has three older siblings who also went to the same school.[4] Everyone wants to be known in their own right.

Andrew brought Simon to Jesus and instantly Simon got all the attention. Even though Andrew was one of the twelve, he wasn't in the inner circle. Jesus' three closest companions and leaders were Simon, James and John. Andrew got bumped by the brother he brought into the group.

How easily Andrew could have descended into self-pity and a massive sulk, thinking it wasn't fair. But he didn't. Equally, how easily Jesus could have included Andrew in the inner three out of a sense of obligation or to save his feelings. But he didn't. And what a good job he didn't!

There are only really two accounts of Andrew's activity in the gospels, and both show something of his character. At the feeding of the 5,000, they were trying to work out what on earth to do with all the hungry people. According to John, it was Andrew who found the boy with the loaves and fish (John 6:8–9). He wasn't in a holy huddle at the front, but out on the edge and engaged.

In a separate incident, some Greeks approached Philip and asked to see Jesus (John 12:22). Philip didn't know what to do, so he asked

---

4 That's not his real surname, but I don't want to embarrass him!

Andrew, who took them to meet Jesus. Again, Andrew was on the edge drawing people in to Jesus.

If Andrew had been among those hanging out closest to Jesus, he would have missed the opportunity to bring others in. We know very little about him, but from what we are told, he was clearly someone who brought those on the edges to Jesus. He didn't huff that he wasn't in the best spot; he took the opportunities that were in front of him. People use up lots of energy when they do what they're not best placed to do. This means that they are then not free to serve in the ways they are meant to, and ways that fit who God has made them to be.

Many of us fail to follow Andrew's lead and, feeling rejected, we put up our defences. The great sadness is that this actually means we are more likely to remain isolated and alone. It also prevents the right people from doing those roles. Just imagine what the Church would be like if we were free from petty jealousies and jostling for position. How great it would be if people were put into roles that suited their gifts and character, and they embraced these positions.

Jay, a friend of mine, once told me about two guys in their twenties who volunteered to help with his youth group (let's call them Pete and Andy). Their church was really passionate about praying into people's God-given design, their gifts and calling. When Pete and Andy had been helping out for a bit, my friend asked Pete to take a few young lads under his wing and disciple them. Pete did a great job and the lads began to flourish.

After this, Jay began to notice that Andy had lost all his enthusiasm and commitment to helping out with the youth. He went to challenge Andy about his attitude, but instead asked him if anything was wrong. Initially Andy said everything was fine, but the conversation progressed and eventually he said he was embarrassed to ask, but wondered if he had done something to upset Jay. Andy confided that he was worried he had done something to make Jay stop trusting him. Jay was totally confused and asked him what had made him feel that way. Andy said he and Pete had joined the team at the same time and some youth had been entrusted to Pete, but none had been entrusted to him.

Jay was shocked. He asked Andy what Pete was best at. Andy quickly said discipleship. Jay then asked what Andy was good at. Andy said he guessed it was evangelism. Jay asked Andy why he would want to disciple church youth when his gifting was as an evangelist. Suddenly it was as though a light went on for Andy. In an instant it all made sense. This whole situation was not about trust or preferential treatment. Andy recognised that had he been given some lads to disciple he would not have known where to even begin. More importantly he would have been drawn into spending all his time in church with the church youth, rather than out on the edges with those outside the church.

The following week Andy turned up to youth group with a beaming smile. The week after, some lads Andy had invited came along. Soon they became Christians. You get the point! We are all different and have different gifts. God wants us to be fully uniquely ourselves, not wishing we were more like someone else or trying to be like them.

Simon Peter

As the gospel writers drew together their individual accounts of Jesus' life they must have had to leave out so much. John says as much, recording that there isn't space to include all that Jesus did (John 21:25). If I was writing a gospel today, one of my top priorities would be making sure that it was an accurate, chronological, historical record. I would definitely add more detail. However, the gospel writers' focus was more thematic and theological. Chronology was less important. Mark's Gospel runs at breakneck speed. He left out anything that wasn't essential and might slow down the narrative.

In Mark's record of Jesus' first encounter with Simon, Simon left everything to follow him. It was so quick. Here is the call of Simon in full:

> As Jesus walked beside the Sea of Galilee, he saw Simon and his brother Andrew casting a net into the lake, for they were fishermen. 'Come, follow me,' Jesus said, 'and I will send you out to fish for people.' At once they left their nets and followed him. (Mark 1:16–18)

We know from other gospel accounts that there was more to it than that. For a start, we know that Andrew had just spent the day with Jesus before bringing Simon to meet him. It seems that since that first meeting, they started hanging together. So much so that after his first public appearance in the synagogue, Jesus went back to Simon's place. While there, he healed Simon's mother-in-law, had dinner and then began to heal all the people who'd gathered outside. He then stayed for a sleepover.

After all this, Jesus was by the Sea of Galilee. He was teaching, and Simon and some others were washing their nets. Jesus realised the crowd was getting big and that he couldn't be heard by everyone. So he got into Simon's boat and continued teaching from the water (Luke 5:1ff.). When he'd finished speaking, he told Simon to push out into deeper water and start fishing. Simon was not convinced. After all, *he* was the professional fisherman – not Jesus. But he recognised the authority of Jesus, called him Teacher and agreed. The catch of fish was so great that Simon didn't bother to count it. He simply fell on his knees at Jesus' feet in recognition of his own sin! Simon no longer called him Teacher, but Lord. It was then that Jesus told him to leave his nets and follow him.

In our time leading a youth church, we spent years working with young people who had little or no interest in God or church. As we told them about the God we knew and loved, we could see some gradually grow in their awareness of him. Later, we would encourage them as they began to live a life of faith. At times, I worried that we weren't very good evangelists. We would spend ages building relationships with these young people as we gradually shared our faith. Some of our friends would just meet people and somehow provoke an immediate decision for Christ. But Simon's story hugely encourages me. In Mark's account, Jesus went walking on the beach, met two fishermen and within one quick conversation they left everything to follow him. Yet their decision was in fact the result of various other experiences and a reasonable amount of time spent with Jesus.

After this, Simon and Jesus spent more and more time together. At some point Jesus spoke prophetically over him, saying that he would be like a rock and should be called Peter (John 1:42). Peter also witnessed Jesus claim a particular prophecy from the Old Testament in his local synagogue (Luke 4:18–19; Isaiah 61). Hundreds of years earlier, the prophet Isaiah had prophesied that God would send someone to proclaim good news to the poor, who would set captives free and help the blind to see. It was a prophecy of hope for a people who felt abandoned by their God. It was a promise that they had not been forgotten and that God would come again and dwell among them.

Jesus claimed that this prophecy was all about him. He was the one they had been waiting for. Peter was with him when he drove out demons and performed the miraculous healing of many people. He heard Jesus teach and saw him overwhelmed by crowds desperate to hear him. He finally worked out who Jesus really was when he, a carpenter, out-fished Peter and his partners. At that moment something shifted for Peter and he recognised Jesus as Lord. It took some time before he recognised him as the long-awaited Messiah.

At this moment Peter also saw himself for who he was. As far as we know, Jesus never underlined how sinful Peter was and how much he needed salvation. Peter understood that for himself.

As Christians, we need to be confident in talking about Jesus. I've heard Archbishop Justin Welby say that, when talking about our faith, we have a thirty-second window in which we have to decide to have the courage to name Jesus rather than avoid doing so. We need to introduce people to him and who he is, rather than hope they'll somehow pick it up for themselves by hanging out with us. Even inviting them to an event connected with church may not be enough. We will actually have to talk about faith and Jesus, and the difference this makes in our lives.

Peter saw the difference Jesus made in the lives of those he encountered. We need to be praying and acting for that to happen today. At the same time, we mustn't be pushy – rushing or manipulating people to make quick decisions. As with Peter, it may take time, but when people truly encounter Jesus, they recognise who he is and their need of him for themselves.

Peter: the external processor

From the outset Peter stood out as the leader of the motley crew of disciples. On the morning after his mother-in-law had been healed, he took a group to find Jesus, who had gone off early to pray (Mark 1:36). It's interesting to see Peter's reactions when a haemorrhaging woman grasped the edge of Jesus' cloak in desperation (Luke 8:45). For twelve years she had been suffering terribly from continuous bleeding.[5] She was instantly and anonymously healed, but Jesus stopped in front of the whole crowd and asked who had touched him. Peter probably voiced the thoughts of many when he responded

---

5   When a Jewish woman was bleeding, she was considered ceremonially unclean. Everything or anyone she touched would be made unclean by her. To become clean again required ritual washing at the end of the day. It would have been easier to avoid all contact with this woman than go to the effort of purification after contact. I might be wrong, but I can only assume she was very lonely. More than this, however, her uncleanness meant she could not attend the Temple, so she was also cut off from God. You can understand her utter desperation for healing after twelve years of living like this.

that there was a crowd, therefore loads of people were touching him all the time.

Peter was not one for false deference. Rather than trying to impress Jesus, Peter was real and honest with him. He was the one who constantly spoke up and said what he was thinking – sometimes unthinkingly. In today's language I think we could confidently describe him as an external processor. I have huge sympathy for Peter, as I am personally aware that those of us who externally process tend to speak a little more often than average! I often wonder whether being quiet is a better life plan. Yet that's not who I am or who Peter was. I do not in any way intend this to be a justification for blurting out unthinking or hurtful words. But it is worth acknowledging that some people will speak first before fully realising the full impact, both positive and negative. As such, the willingness to speak up, to put your opinion forward, can be both a strength and a weakness.

Peter: recognising who Jesus is

Sometime later Jesus asked who people were saying he was (Matthew 16:13). The disciples were quick to respond with various perspectives. But when Jesus extended the question and asked who *they* said he was, it was a far more vulnerable thing to risk an answer. Unsurprisingly, it was Peter who spoke up. His answer was: 'You are the Messiah, the Son of the living God' (verse 16). He was completely right. In fact, his answer was so good, Jesus said that he couldn't have got to it on his own. Poor Peter!

Finally, we see Peter saying the right thing at the right time and Jesus says he could only have got it right if God had shown him. I wonder if he was a bit discouraged by that, wanting at least some credit. But Jesus was telling Peter a brilliant truth that applies to us all. Only God can reveal himself to us. Understanding who God is doesn't come down to our intellectual brilliance. God can reveal himself to the brightest and the not so bright. It is also perfectly possible that, however much we think we understand, we can still miss the point. God doesn't conform to our expectations. Peter understood who Jesus was, but didn't understand what that truly meant. In fact, Jesus defied all his expectations and understandings of God and his Messiah. In the very next paragraph, when Jesus described his inevitable suffering, Peter strongly refuted it and said it must never happen (verse 22). It was inconceivable to him that Jesus might suffer and die. Jesus turned and said, 'Get behind me, Satan! You are a stumbling block to me; you do not have in mind the concerns of God, but merely human concerns' (verse 23).

In one breath Peter was hailed as the rock on which the Church would be built; in the next he was rebuked like Satan. Within moments he went from getting it astoundingly right to shockingly wrong. God held this tension with no trouble. We find holding this tension far harder. When we get it wrong, or mess up, we struggle to still believe that God can trust us or use us. We ask if God really can love us when we constantly misunderstand him and need correcting. But clearly he can. He is bigger than any of our failures. God entrusted the leadership and direction of the Church to someone from whose mouth came divine insights and the perspectives of Satan! So I'm pretty sure he can also use you and me.

It is interesting that Luke recorded Peter's declaration of faith but spared him the embarrassment of his error and the rebuke that followed (Luke 9:18ff.). Matthew included the rebuke but played down Peter's foot-in-mouth moment. Mark, normally the most succinct, included everything (Mark 8:27ff.). This is significant, because his gospel is most probably based on Peter's recollections. He seems to have told the story to Mark as it was, rather than trying to present himself in a better light. He was happy to be recorded in the gospels as one who messed up yet loved wholeheartedly.

Simon Peter: speak first, think later

Just over a week after Peter declared who Jesus was, Jesus took only Peter, James and John on a special outing. This wasn't the first occasion that these three had been singled out. Peter, James and John were also present when Jesus raised a little girl from the dead.[6] They were taken up a mountain to pray with Jesus. And as Jesus prayed he was transfigured. He began to radiate divine glory, like Moses. Then Moses and Elijah were there with him. This was a holy moment, a moment when Jesus talked with Moses of his forthcoming 'exodus' for the salvation of the world. Moses and Elijah represented the 'law and the prophets', the whole of Jewish identity, history and future hope. They were symbolically meeting across space and time to discuss what Jesus had come to accomplish once and for all.

At this awesome event Peter interrupted, saying what a relief they had brought him because he could sort out somewhere for each of them to sleep. As Mark helpfully points out, 'He did not know what to say, they were so frightened' (Mark 9:6). Oh, Peter!

Peter has my fullest sympathy. He didn't know what to say, but he had to say something. Some people won't understand him, but others of us have found a soulmate! A friend once told me that he had learned there was never a moment too serious or sacred for me to make a silly comment. I'd like to think that he was being encouraging, but I'm not completely certain! Like me, Peter never held back on what he was thinking. He was all in, in every situation.

At the transfiguration Peter was obviously overwhelmed. There was another moment in Jesus' ministry when the disciples began to realise the full extent of what it meant to follow him. For some this was just too much, and disciples stopped following him (John 6:66ff.). Noticing this, Jesus asked whether the apostles were going to leave too. Peter responded on their behalf, asking who else they

---

6 This was Jairus's daughter, as told in Mark 5:21–43. The story surrounds the one of the haemorrhaging woman. It is officially called a 'Markan sandwich' but is of interest, as the two stories are meant to be read together. Note that the twelve-year-old girl was important in society because of her dad, and the woman who had suffered for twelve years was written off by society, yet alongside her healing was called daughter.

would go to. He went on to acknowledge that Jesus was the Holy One of God, he was offering eternal life, and there was no one else they would rather follow and nowhere else they would choose to be.

If Jesus was teaching and Peter didn't understand, he instantly came straight back at Jesus. He would jump right in with his questions if a parable made no sense to him, even if it made him look a bit dim (Matthew 15:15). When Jesus taught about what to do when someone hurts you, it was Peter who came back later to clarify how many times he might have to forgive. He asked if it could possibly be as many as seven times.[7] When Jesus had been saying that money wouldn't get you into the kingdom and that you couldn't save yourself, Peter was upset and confused. He asked what they'd get for giving up everything to follow Jesus (Matthew 19:27). But for all his bluster and unthinking words, Peter was humble before God. He wanted to understand.

It's good to question and challenge, but it can also be dangerous. We can easily move from questioning to putting ourselves in judgement over God and the Scriptures. When God acts in Scripture in ways we find unreasonable or difficult it is tempting to try and force God into an image of how we would like him to be. But then God becomes an idol of our own making. Instead, we must approach God with humility, recognising that we will never fully understand. It is good to probe and want to understand, but at the same time we need to hold on to the fact that we are very limited in our understanding.

Peter: getting out of the boat

One of the most extraordinary nights of Peter's life must have been when he walked on water (Matthew 14:22–33). After the feeding of 5,000, Jesus sent the disciples back in a boat while he sorted

---

7 Jesus took it to a whole different level by saying it was seventy times seven times. Seven was seen as the number representing completion, so this was the most extreme expectation (Matthew 18:21–35).

the crowd out and then went off to pray. It was a windy night and, as morning approached, Jesus walked on the water over to the disciples' boat. They thought it was a ghost, but eventually they worked out that it was Jesus. Peter requested that Jesus call him on to the water too. Jesus said, 'Come!' Peter got out of the boat and began to make his way to Jesus, walking on the water.

It all went well until he stopped for just a moment, realised exactly what he was doing and promptly began to sink. As soon as he looked at how bad the storm was rather than looking at Jesus, he began to sink. Peter cried out to Jesus to save him and he simply reached out his hand and caught him. Jesus then said, 'You of little faith, why did you doubt?' I know that I read this as Peter having messed it up yet again. He's doubted, failed and needed rescuing.

So many Christians today hold off stepping out of the boat in case they get it wrong and fail. We can be unwilling to step out in prayer, expressing faith, because we fear the disappointment of our prayer not being answered. We don't know how far Peter made it before he began to sink, but the fact remains that he did walk on water. Not many humans can make that claim. In fact, he walked far enough that, when he began to sink, Jesus could simply hold out his hand to reach him. He made it all the way to Jesus and only at that point began to think about the craziness of what he was doing. Once Jesus had grabbed his hand, he must also have then walked back to the boat with him to be able to get into it.

When you picture Jesus and Peter returning to the boat hand in hand, it adds a very different tone to Jesus' challenge about his lack of faith. I love that you are unlikely to be harshly rebuking someone while walking along hand in hand.[8] Jesus' words are expressed with love, not condemnation or accusation. There is such a fine line between failure and success. Peter walked on water! He may well have stumbled, but he still did it. We will miss out on what God has

---

8 I know the text doesn't say that they walked along holding hands, but I don't really believe Peter would have let go and kept walking!

for us if we're too scared of getting it wrong. But if we try – and get it wrong – Jesus doesn't rebuke us; he gently challenges us for more.

Jesus doesn't struggle under the circumstances of our lives. He is greater than them, not weighed down by them. We need to actively give God permission to stretch our faith and broaden our horizons. It's central to discipleship that we keep stepping out in faith as Peter did.

Peter: all in and then all out

Peter's full-on passion came to the fore at the Last Supper (John 13:6ff.). Before they ate, Jesus took on the role of a servant and started to wash the feet of his disciples. It was a lowly task, and I'm guessing a smelly one. When Jesus got to Peter, Peter couldn't conceive of Jesus demeaning himself so much, and adamantly refused. Jesus told Peter that he was not understanding Jesus' ministry, and that if he didn't let him wash his feet, then he, Peter, had no part of him. Peter instantly underwent a complete reversal and asked to be washed completely. Peter's passion is inspiring, but it's not enough. It can't be equated with being deeply committed.

When Jesus said his disciples would all fall away, Peter vehemently responded that everyone else may fall but he never would (Matthew 26:33). He saw himself as better than the rest. But this was not the case. He would struggle just as much as the rest of the disciples, running away as they did. The only ones who wouldn't run were the women. Not only would Peter run away, but he would explicitly deny Jesus.

Some people are naturally exuberant and passionate. Others are more reserved and reticent. Often the passionate ones are assumed to be the most full of faith. But those with huge outward energy and excitement can be struggling with doubt just as much on the inside as anyone else.

I know a young married couple who ticked all the boxes. They were beautiful, talented, fun, godly and intelligent. They were always asked to lead things at their church and used as role models for others. One day, the wife shocked me by saying how much she struggled with church. She said that everyone assumed all was great with them because they looked OK on the outside. (In fact, they didn't look OK, they looked stunning, but fortunately I didn't correct her.) She shared with me that she was struggling with her faith, life and identity, but no one ever checked she was all right, and it felt as if she was being split in two. It's so easy to make assumptions based on external appearances. Fortunately God doesn't do that. As this book hopefully illustrates, we all have our struggles, weaknesses and insecurities.

Praying against temptation

Jesus not only warned Peter that he would deny him three times, but he also said that Satan was after the disciples. Jesus said that he had prayed Peter wouldn't fail and that when he returned he must strengthen his brothers (Luke 22:30–32). After supper, the disciples and Jesus went out to Gethsemane. Jesus told them to pray that they wouldn't fall into temptation. He went a little distance from them and prayed earnestly to the point of sweating blood.[9] Jesus was deeply distressed, yet when he returned to them, he found all the disciples asleep. He again told them to pray that they wouldn't fall into temptation. At first glance we might assume that the temptation they were supposed to avoid is falling asleep when praying and thus failing to support Jesus in his hour of need. It's far more likely that Jesus was encouraging them to pray for themselves as Satan aimed to attack their faith over the coming hours and days. This was far more vital.

For Peter, the real temptation was not to sleep, but to deny Christ. Jesus had prayed that his faith wouldn't fail, but Peter

---

9 Scientists now recognise this as a physiological phenomenon induced by extreme anguish. See J. E. Holoubek and A. B. Holoubek, 'Blood, sweat and fear. "A classification of hematidrosis"'. *Journal of Medicine*, 1996, 27(3–4): 115–33. PMID: 8982961.

needed to pray as well. Jesus knew that a far greater danger for Peter than the initial denial was that his failure would cause him to abandon his faith.

I can't tell you what percentage of my prayer over the years has been praying about my praying. Countless times I've sat down to pray and then spent most of my prayer time apologising for my lack of prayer in previous days. Or I'll start to pray and then get distracted or, worse still, doze off. I then spend the rest of the time praying about that. Satan has nothing to fear in our prayers if they focus on the act of prayer rather than on what we need to pray about. Jesus was calling the disciples to pray to prepare themselves for the most unimaginable time ahead. Staying awake was nothing compared with that.

If the devil can't distract us from prayer by focusing on the poverty of our prayer, he can deflect us on to cyclical prayers of regret and guilt. Jesus warned Peter of this. It's why he prayed for Peter's return after failing, so that Peter didn't give up.

There is no condemnation in Christ. Condemnation doesn't lead to repentance and to Christ; it drags us down into despair. It doesn't matter if our prayers are stumbling and inarticulate, or even if they are not as frequent as they should be. What matters is that we are turning our hearts and attention to God, and opening ourselves to him and his purposes.

The verses that undergirded the vision of Unlimited were Hebrews 12:1–2: 'Let us throw off everything that hinders and the sin that so easily entangles. And let us run with perseverance the race marked out for us, fixing our eyes on Jesus, the pioneer and perfecter of faith.' Prayer is the constant tearing of our attention off other things to focus our eyes on him, and it is vital.

Arrest and denial

As I've already said, there were no shades of grey with Peter – he was all in or all out. He was impulsive and full of passion. When a Roman guard came to arrest Jesus, Peter grabbed his sword and tried to protect Jesus from arrest. He had no hope in the face of the formidable force of Rome, but it didn't hold him back. Admittedly, he did show some sense, since he lashed out at the softest option: the high priest's servant. But Peter, even in the face of a hopeless situation, wasn't willing to stand by and let it happen. We don't know how many disciples followed after Jesus was arrested, but Peter certainly did (John 18:15ff.). He bravely entered the courtyard of the high priest's house. Three times he was accused of being one of Jesus' followers and each time he denied it. On the final denial, Jesus looked directly at him.

This sounds a bit harsh on Jesus' part, but maybe the intensity and devastation of this failure was what made Peter the leader he would become. In that instant he rushed outside and wept bitterly, but he returned for the crucifixion. He ran away, but he came back. This is a key indicator of his heart.

Peter's restoration

Peter was there for Jesus' death and with the other apostles in the upper room for the ensuing days. When the women found the empty tomb, Peter went running to see it for himself. In fact, he was the first to enter, rushing in headlong as always! We can't imagine what it must have been like for Peter to sit around with the other disciples, facing the devastation of Jesus' death and his 'failure' prior to the resurrection. Jesus then appeared twice to them after the resurrection, and hope must have begun to grow.[10] Yet they still didn't get it. Following his denials, this must have been hard for Peter. He must have questioned his ability to lead if he was no better than the rest of them. Yet this is not how Jesus seems to view leadership. Peter was not called by Jesus because he had it all together and never failed.

10 In fact, according to Luke 24:34, he also appeared to Peter on his own.

One evening Peter announced he was going fishing. With his type of all-in personality, he must have been going crazy cooped up in a room. The others decided to go with him, so Peter's outing to get away turned into a fishing trip with more than half the apostles (John 21:2). They fished all night and caught nothing. If I were Peter, it would have compounded all my dark thoughts: I can't lead for Jesus, and I can't go back to my day job because I'm useless at that too. Then a voice echoed out from the shore asking if they'd caught any fish. When they said they hadn't, the man told them to try the other side. They did as he suggested. Was it because of their tiredness, the authority of the instruction or the familiarity of the voice they'd learned to listen to and obey?

The size of their catch overwhelmed them. One of the disciples, 'the disciple whom Jesus loved', realised they'd been here before and that it was Jesus. This disciple declared that it was the Lord and, in an instant, Peter was pulled from his melancholy. He grabbed his coat and jumped into the water and rushed to be with Jesus. It's a weird detail to say that he grabbed his coat, but maybe it illustrates that he wasn't coming back to fishing ever again. From then on for Peter, it was Jesus all the way and nothing else.

When he reached the shore, Jesus asked for some fish, so Peter rushed back to the boat to get him some. In the meantime, one of them counted the fish. There were 153. As true fishermen, there was no way that they would let the size of the catch go unknown! When Jesus performed the same miracle at the beginning of the gospels, immediately before calling them to follow him, they had not thought to count the fish. They weren't making that mistake a second time! They wanted to know how big the miracle was.

Jesus rustled up some breakfast for them. At this point, Peter had denied Jesus three times. But over breakfast, Jesus turned to him and asked three times if he loved him. Each time he responded that he did, Jesus asked him to feed or care for his sheep/lambs. In so doing, Jesus restored him.

We all fail and let God down and that is always forgivable. We will make mistakes and even deny our faith and our Lord, but what matters most is that we love him. As we saw previously, Saul and David both failed. By human understanding, David's failures were way more serious. But ultimately David loved God and wanted to follow him, even if he didn't always live up to that desire. Peter also loved Jesus deeply and passionately, but he didn't always come through. And that was OK. Jesus' only concern was that he loved him. When he was certain that he did, Jesus happily entrusted the feeding and care of his beloved sheep to Peter.

There is an odd ending to this tale. Just when Jesus had spoken restoration over Peter three times, Peter got distracted. We should expect it by now. This time, just as Jesus was looking him in the eyes and speaking of love, Peter caught a glimpse of one of the other disciples – the one referred to as 'the disciple whom Jesus loved'. He asked, 'Oh, Jesus, what about him?' Jesus basically said that it was none of his business. All Peter needed to worry about was following Jesus himself (John 21:22). It's another reminder that we mustn't waste our energy comparing ourselves to others, making ourselves feel either better or worse. Although Christian faith is all about community and is not individualistic, in this respect we must focus on ourselves. We are ultimately only responsible for ensuring we follow Jesus the best we can. If we spend all our time looking over our shoulder at others, we will only trip up.

Peter's story continues into the book of Acts. He was a man who was totally devoted in his heart, but didn't always get it right. In Acts he had an argument with God about what food he could eat. Later Peter was told off by Paul for being hypocritical out of fear of offending people. He remained the one who spoke, often before thinking. Some things never change. Yet he was also the one Jesus chose to lead the Church. His first recorded sermon brought 3,000 to faith. Jesus knew what he was doing.

James and John: the Sons of Thunder

Immediately after Simon Peter and Andrew had left their nets and started following Jesus, Jesus called James and John. They were fishermen too. They promptly left their dad, Zebedee, and followed Jesus. As Simon was quickly rebranded as Peter, Jesus gave James and John the new name 'Sons of Thunder' (Mark 3:17). I'm not sure that their new nickname was complimentary! I thought Jesus was all about drawing the best out of people and having a growth mindset. But sometimes the best thing we can do is to be honest. It's better than the toxic niceness we sometimes see in church, when people pretend everything is great to someone's face and then moan behind their back. We attempt to keep a healthy distance rather than confront their behaviour. I'm not recommending labelling people by their weaknesses, but Jesus knew what he was doing here. I also think that he was calling them to something better. In acknowledging their inherited trait of anger, he was inviting them to own it and aspire to more.

A while ago, I went on some training that talked about our 'shadow side' – the darker things within us that we try to repress. It was explained that we can sometimes see our shadow by looking at what we react against in others. I immediately recognised two things that I react against: when people speak brazenly about things that could be seen as undignified to discuss and when people are blatantly ambitious. Interestingly, I recognised during the training that I had become increasingly irritated with two people because of these two behaviours. They were things that I don't like, so when I saw them in myself, I repressed rather than owned them. We need to own things that are not right in our lives and bring them to God rather than avoid them.

James and John were called by Jesus and left their dad behind, but they couldn't leave behind their anger. We see it in full force when a Samaritan village refused to welcome Jesus (Luke 9:54).

The Sons of Thunder asked Jesus if they should call fire down from heaven to destroy the people! Awkwardly, this is one of their only two speaking parts in the gospels. The other involves their mum and is probably even more significant.

It is later in the gospels as James and John recognised that things were coming to a head. The end was beginning to feel near. When Jesus took his place in his kingdom, they wanted to be there on either side of him. They wanted the best seats. They wanted status. So they put in their clumsy request.

Just as Jesus had finished vividly describing the torture he would experience at his death, James and John piped up with their request (Mark 10:32–45). It was as if they hadn't been listening to a word Jesus was saying. Jesus was talking vulnerably about the horror of his impending death, and James and John blundered in. Although it's worth noting that in Matthew's Gospel the request was made by their mum (Matthew 20:20–21).

Jesus told them that they didn't know what they were talking about. He asked whether they were willing to suffer as he would. They declared that they were. Jesus replied that they could suffer, but they couldn't have the best seats. Bit harsh, maybe? Why did he ask about suffering only to say that they couldn't have the seats? Probably because the two were linked. They wanted the glory, but throughout John's Gospel Jesus' place of glory is the cross. So to be on his left and right as he went into glory was to be on either side of him at the cross. But those places on either side of Jesus' cross were already taken by the thieves.

The other disciples were 'indignant' at James and John. They were upset that they hadn't managed to ask first and were worried they would miss out.[11] The disciples had so much to learn. The last time Jesus had been 'indignant' was when children were kept from him as though they were of less value (Mark 10:14). The disciples

---

11 It's a bit like in our church, where people used to call 'Shotgun!' to reserve the favourite seat first. It used to really annoy me!

got indignant when their sense of value or worth was challenged. Jesus' indignation was about the valuing of others; the disciples' indignation was about valuing themselves.

Jesus then took the disciples to one side to encourage them that in God's eyes value doesn't come from position or status. This is also revealing for us. What makes us indignant? Do we get indignant when our value or position is challenged? Or when people are hindered from being brought to Jesus? The Church would be very different if the latter was our greatest concern.

Jesus called James and John Sons of Thunder recognising some of their weaknesses, but also drawing them in as his closest friends. They were in the inner three with Peter. On several occasions, such as for the transfiguration, it was only Peter, James and John he took with him. Jesus loved them with their faults and not for anything they achieved.

In John's Gospel (probably written by this John of 'James and John') there is a character referred to as 'the disciple whom Jesus loved' (John 13:23; 21:7 and so on). We've mentioned him twice already, when Jesus helped them bring in an almighty fish haul after his resurrection and when Peter got distracted and asked Jesus what would happen to another disciple. As always, theologians have plenty of theories about who this was. In John 21:24, John implies that it is himself.

Admittedly, referring to himself as 'the disciple whom Jesus loved' could be seen as the ultimate grasping of status, or arrogance. Alternatively, it could be seen as the ultimate expression of wonder. His statement was not about comparison. He was not bragging that he was the one Jesus loved more than the rest. It was just a statement of the fact that he was loved. His name no longer mattered. What mattered was that Jesus could love *him*.

John, the Son of Thunder, who once wanted to call down fire to destroy a city, may also have been the author of three letters in the Bible: 1, 2 and 3 John. In them, one of his favourite forms of address is 'Beloved' and one of his overriding themes is love. Jesus' love completely transformed him. With Jesus, he discovered what it was to be loved – 'be-loved'. We are God's beloved disciples whom Jesus loves too. Regardless of our experiences of love, or the lack of it, in our past or present, Jesus offers to heal us with his love.

Philip

Another early recruit was Philip. He was from the same town as Andrew and Peter: Bethsaida. As John recorded it, one day Jesus called Andrew and Peter and then the next day, as he was about to set off for Galilee, he called Philip. A bit like Andrew, Philip's first act as a new disciple was to grab someone else to bring along. He rushed off to Nathanael and said that he had found the one whom Moses and the prophets had spoken about – Jesus of Nazareth. Nathanael was unconvinced and said that nothing good could come from Nazareth. Philip brilliantly didn't argue with him; he just told him to come and see. This is a fantastic model for sharing our faith. Rather than trying to argue with people, we can just invite them to come along and see Jesus.

The next time we see Philip is at the feeding of the 5,000 (John 6:5). According to John, Jesus turned to Philip and asked where they could buy bread for the people to eat. Jesus already had a plan, but wanted to test Philip. Philip responded that it would take more than half a year's wages to buy enough for everyone to have a bite. We don't hear how he scored in the test. I'm guessing not very well. He was saved by Andrew bringing along the boy with the loaves and fish at that moment.

Philip's next cameo appearance may be similar (John 12:21ff.). Some Greeks asked Philip if they could see Jesus, and his response was to turn to Andrew and tell him about the request. They then both went to Jesus. It was almost as if Andrew rescued him again. Or at least gave him the confidence to go to Jesus with the request.

Poor Philip. He doesn't seem to have been the most confident disciple!

Towards the end of Jesus' life, he gave some of his most profound teaching. The Gospel of John records Jesus disclosing that the only way to the Father was through him. He went on to say that if the disciples really knew him, they would also know his Father. In fact, he said that from now on they 'do know him and have seen him' (John 14:7). As if he wasn't completely listening, Philip interjected, 'Lord, show us the Father and that will be enough for us.' Jesus asked, 'Don't you know me, Philip, even after I have been among you such a long time? Anyone who has seen me has seen the Father. How can you say, "Show us the Father"?' (verse 9).

On the one hand, it seems that Philip was being a bit slow. On the other hand, even after all these centuries, the Trinity is still something we struggle to get our heads around. If I'm honest, I feel for Philip. I think he'd have been safer to keep quiet. Yet isn't it good that he asked a question that elicited such a great answer from Jesus? The response helps us understand the mystery of the Trinity better ourselves. Also, isn't it so encouraging that we can come to God with our questions, however great or dim they are?

Jesus' disciple Philip is only recorded in John's Gospel and he doesn't come out that well. He seemed to either need Andrew's help, or to ask a question that Jesus had already answered. But in our age when children are scrutinised and pressured to get good grades for fear of being labelled stupid or worthless, Philip shows that there is more to life than our intellectual prowess. Like Andrew, he met people on the edges and brought them in. The first time we meet him, he is bringing someone to Jesus. He didn't try to win Nathanael around intellectually. He didn't need to. He just took him to Jesus. Jesus doesn't just call the intellectually impressive or those with the gift of the gab. He looks to our heart and draws us to his.

Bartholomew

Bartholomew appears in the list of the twelve apostles in Matthew, Mark and Luke. He was also in the upper room after Jesus ascended to heaven. Other than that, there is no record of him in the Bible. So I could just leave him there. But there is a theory that he had a second name, as with some of the other apostles. Each time he is listed in the gospels he appears in the list next to Philip and we know that Philip brought Nathanael to Jesus. Was Bartholomew also known as Nathanael? There is no mention of Bartholomew in John's Gospel, but there are several mentions of Nathanael.

Nathanael was the one we just met with Philip. The first thing we hear him say is that nothing good could come out of Nazareth. He almost rejected the Messiah because of his geographical origins. That's a bit like saying nothing good could come out of Plymouth or from up north.[12] But at least he was willing to put his prejudice aside long enough to find out more.

When he approached Jesus, Jesus greeted him slightly strangely, saying, 'Here truly is an Israelite in whom there is no deceit' (John 1:47). Even more strangely, from just these few words Nathanael asked how he knew him. There was no false modesty with Nathanael! Rather than complimenting him, perhaps Jesus had just expressed the quality he was best known for.

Jesus went on to say that he saw where Nathanael was sitting, under a fig tree, before Philip called him. It wasn't that Jesus had clocked him as he walked past. This was divine revelation. There might even have been a twinkle in his eye as he said it. Nathanael dismissed where Jesus came from, so Jesus told him where he had

---

12 Plymouth has recently been recognised as one of the UK's most underrated destinations. It has the spectacular waterfront of the Hoe and historical charm of the Barbican. It has centuries of naval history, including a famous bowls match with the Spanish Armada. It is great for sea swimming, with Britain's finest seawater lido. There is The Box, a fantastic gallery and museum, the Theatre Royal and three universities. I could go on. There are good things about the north too!

come from. Jesus knows us completely. When he calls us to follow him, he knows exactly where we've been.

One of my colleagues has a sticker with a picture of Jesus saying, 'I saw that.' The other day three of us were discussing it. I said that I really didn't like it; it made me think of the worst kind of school assembly, where children were told to behave, with the added threat that Jesus was watching. My colleague saw it as Jesus watching more like an attentive parent. He was keeping a watching, caring eye. The other person added that there was huge encouragement for them that Jesus misses nothing. We can do something brave or generous that goes unnoticed by everyone else, but God sees it. The conversation totally changed my perspective on the sticker. All too easily, even though theologically I know it's not true, my default is to assume that God looks at my actions and attitude with disappointment rather than care and love.

In two short statements Jesus showed that he knew Nathanael's character and his origins. It was enough for Nathanael to make possibly the boldest declaration in the gospels: that Jesus was both the Son of God and King of Israel. Jesus then declared that Nathanael would have a vision like Jacob's, only it would include Jesus (Genesis 28:12). This might be Jesus saying that Nathanael would be there for his ascension, or that Nathanael would see something of heaven poured out on Jesus in his life.

Nathanael was there with Peter when he went fishing and Jesus appeared to them. It seems strange that he would be fishing with six of the apostles if he wasn't one himself. Therefore, either Nathanael was indeed Bartholomew, or he was one of Jesus' core disciples but not included in the twelve. What a shame to be so close to Jesus and not have your name recorded consistently! But the lack of clarity about his name or who he was doesn't diminish what he experienced and knew of Jesus. Surely it is so much more important to know Jesus and live for him than to get the credit for it.

Thomas aka Doubting Thomas

After he left school, one of our sons told us the nickname he had been given in sport. It wasn't the most flattering, but he was pleased to be given a nickname at all.[13] To him it showed that they cared enough about him to bother to name him – plus, for teenage lads, taking the mick out of each other can be the equivalent of a giant hug. But having a nickname isn't always positive. Throughout history, Thomas has been known as Doubting Thomas. I think this is unfair and misses so much of his character and faith.

Philip asked Jesus to show them the Father but, just before this, Thomas also asked a question. Jesus said, 'You know the way to the place where I am going' (John 14:4ff.), to which Thomas responded, 'Lord, we don't know where you are going, so how can we know the way?' It was a fair question, because until Jesus explained, there was no way they could have known. Thomas's question then led on to one of the most significant statements Jesus ever made: that he is the way, the truth and the life.

Some of us would rather keep quiet than ask a question like Thomas. We're too afraid to expose ourselves and our ignorance. We nod along, pretending to agree and understand rather than ask questions or show our confusion. But it is healthier to be honest and admit we don't have a clue. We are unlikely to be alone in our incomprehension. I was in a meeting recently where I asked a question gently challenging something the speaker had said. It was a tumbleweed moment. No one else backed me up or seemed to echo my question or concern. The speaker, as I'd anticipated, was quite dismissive of what I'd raised. On three occasions later that week, I met people who'd been at the meeting and thanked me for what I'd said. It turned out I had put into words what other

---

13 I know you've only turned to this footnote to find out what the nickname was. I'm sorry to disappoint you, but I embarrass my children enough without letting on what their nicknames are. Also, Josh is over six feet, so I'm not willing to upset him. Sorry!

people were wrestling with. We need to be careful not to assume that because we think something everyone else must be thinking the same, but there are times when we need to have the courage to voice things others may not be able to.

Thomas's greater moment of honesty came after Jesus had died. On the evening of the first day of the week, Jesus appeared in the upper room to his disciples. Disappointingly, Thomas wasn't there. It's so annoying when you wait in for a parcel and pop out just at the moment when the courier comes by! But this was on a whole other level. The disciples were locked in the upper room in fear. It would have been a massive thing for Thomas to go out. I don't imagine it happened much. And Jesus chose that moment to appear to the disciples. All the other apostles were there. The only one missing was Thomas.

When he returned, the other disciples excitedly told him what he'd missed and he retorted, 'Unless I see the nail marks in his hands and put my finger where the nails were, and put my hand into his side, I will not believe' (John 20:25). OK, it wasn't the best response, but if I were him, I'd have been in a giant sulk at the time. Moodiness aside, it was a reasonable reaction. None of them expected Jesus to rise again. In fact they expected the opposite – that it was all over. There must have been a lot of confusion in the room after the empty tomb was discovered. If one of the others had missed it, they may well have thought the same. But thanks to Thomas's expression of doubt, we have a great rebuttal to those who challenge the validity of what the disciples saw. For a start, Thomas wasn't there and he wasn't caught up in emotion. Instead he was actively questioning it.

Poor Thomas had to wait a whole week in the agony of not knowing. Jesus then appeared again. Seven whole days later. Having greeted them all, Jesus turned to Thomas and told him to touch his wounds and to stop doubting and believe. But in that moment, Thomas didn't need to touch him to be convinced. He proclaimed

Jesus as his Lord and his God. He was the first to explicitly call Jesus God. What a fantastic declaration of faith! Jesus did say that Thomas believed because he saw Jesus, and that those, like us, who don't see and yet believe are even more blessed. This is another huge encouragement for those of us who struggle at times in our faith. Jesus recognises that it is harder to believe having not seen. And to be fair to Thomas, the other disciples didn't necessarily believe until they had seen either.

Perspective changes everything. I've always thought how harsh it was that Jesus chose the moment Thomas was absent to appear to the disciples. Then he made him wait a whole seven days before appearing again. Recently I heard someone speak movingly of Jesus' love for each of us as individuals. They illustrated it by saying that they thought Jesus only appeared the second time for Thomas's sake – for the one. Just as he appeared on the road to Emmaus for the two. Isn't it amazing how we can see the same incident from totally different perspectives? Either Jesus didn't care about Thomas by coming when he wasn't there, or he cared so much that he came simply for Thomas's benefit.

But I have skipped over Thomas's other appearance in the gospels. When news reached Jesus that his close friend Lazarus was ill, he decided to return to Judea to be with him (John 11). The disciples all turned on Jesus, saying that there was no way he could return to Judea. They reminded him that only a short time ago, the Jews had tried to stone him to death there. But Jesus was determined. He had to go.

The disciples were unconvinced and it was Thomas who argued against all the others. He boldly declared that they should go with Jesus to die with him. He didn't dispute that going to Lazarus could end in death, but that wasn't a reason not to go. Thomas may not have been quick to believe or commit, but as soon as he was convinced of something, he was willing to follow through, even till death. Processing things carefully and making considered decisions rather than leaping in can be good. What is undeniable was Thomas's commitment to his faith. He was ready to die with and for Jesus.

Just as a little aside: several times John's Gospel says 'Thomas also known as Didymus'. Didymus means 'twin', as does Thomas. So, weirdly, he was called Twin Twin. We have two pairs of brothers following Jesus, James and John and Andrew and Peter, but there is no sign of Thomas's twin. How sad. This is also, in a sense, reassuring. Even with Jesus, God incarnate, right in front of them, not everyone followed him. So we shouldn't be discouraged when people don't respond to him today.

Matthew and Simon

There is only one account of Matthew in the New Testament. Unsurprisingly it's in his gospel – the Gospel of Matthew. Jesus spotted him at work and called Matthew to follow him (Matthew 9:9ff.). Awkwardly, Matthew was a tax collector. Tax collectors were among the lowest of the low in Jewish society, on a level with prostitutes. They aided and abetted Roman occupation, making a tidy profit for themselves at the expense of their fellow people. They were traitors. Jews also believed that tributes should only be paid to God, so taxation was a form of blasphemy.

Yet Jesus went to Matthew's house for dinner. This drew criticism from the Pharisees, but Jesus' response was that the healthy don't need a doctor. Jesus knew that he had not come for the righteous, but for the sinners. This is where the Bible would be better as a film. The written word misses the hint of sarcasm in Jesus' tone. All of us need Jesus. However much we might think we are healthy or righteous, we aren't. We all need salvation. Having a tax collector among the twelve highlights that Jesus came to save anyone and everyone. Just as no one is without need of rescue, no one is beyond rescue. In fact, Jesus showed positive discrimination to those whom the religious of his day would have written off. They were his dinner companions of choice. I'm not sure that can be said of many church leaders today.

I don't know if you've ever been in a team where two people just don't get on and seemingly never will. Jesus not only invited a tax collector to join him, but at the same time also invited a zealot, Simon. A zealot was basically a terrorist. Zealots justified religious acts of violence and aggression as defending the faith. They did everything they could to disrupt and undermine the Roman rule. So within Jesus' small and perfectly formed crack team, there was someone collaborating with the Romans and someone trying to overthrow them – a traitor and a terrorist.

We assume that Matthew wouldn't have wanted to be left in a room on his own with Simon. Not only would there have been immense enmity between them, but also few would hold any hope of redemption for these two. However, within the twelve Jesus showed that he could bring unity between anyone and transformation to everyone. The twelve were a microcosm of the Church. As the New Testament showed, church would bring together the least likely people: male and female; slave and free; Jew and Gentile. Heaven will contain every type of person. No one is beneath or beyond inclusion. I am challenged about how radically inclusive our churches are. I'm also not sure how much we break down division and labelling rather than reinforce it.

Interestingly, Matthew had another name, Levi, which is how Mark and Luke refer to him. Both names mean 'gift of God'. Even the worst of sinners is a gift of God. I wonder when Simon the zealot came to see that.

Judas Iscariot

I guess it's time we came to the black sheep of the apostles, Judas. Judas, the one who betrayed Jesus. Even before his ultimate act of betrayal, all was not well with Judas. When Mary poured nard all over Jesus' feet, Judas objected (John 12:1ff.). Judas condemned the act as wasteful, because the perfume could have been sold and the money given to the poor. Yet his concern was far more likely to have been about the value of the perfume itself than anything to do with compassion for the poor.

As John explains, Judas was a thief (John 12:6). He looked after the money bag and used to help himself to it. Jesus the Son of God, who was without sin, chose a thief not only to join his trusted apostles, but also to take charge of the money. He made this choice after a night in prayer seeking his Father's wisdom about which twelve to choose. That's encouraging to those of us who have made bad team appointments. Jesus didn't choose the perfect team. There was space for failure within God's economy (pun intended!), even among those entrusted with starting the Church.

We'll never know why Judas betrayed Jesus. Some say that he became disillusioned when he saw that Jesus wasn't going to take on the Romans. Others say it was to force Jesus' hand, to make him clearly reveal himself as the Messiah so that he could bring in the kingdom in all its glory. I'd like to think that there may have been some good motives behind what he did, even if it led him to make terrible decisions. It's hard to believe that following Jesus for three years didn't have some positive effect on Judas. But we can never know about his full motives, and sadly Scripture gives no indication of him trying to act as a catalyst for the kingdom. That theory is pure conjecture.

What Scripture does tell us is that Judas was a thief who betrayed Jesus for money. He went to the chief priests and asked them what they would give him for handing Jesus over to them (Matthew 26:14ff.). They offered him thirty pieces of silver. Judas accepted and then waited for his opportunity.

Satan was also involved.[14] Luke talks about Satan entering Judas as he went to meet the chief priests and teachers of the law (Luke

---

14 We last talked about him in David's calling of a census.

22:3). John says that the devil had already prompted him to betray Jesus (John 13:2). Then, as he took the bread from Jesus at the Last Supper, Satan entered him (verse 27). This seems complicated and unfair, but what we do know is that although Satan was undeniably involved, Judas still had responsibility for his actions.

In Ephesians Paul talks about not giving Satan a foothold in our lives (Ephesians 4:27). The Greek word for foothold was also used by Jesus to refer to the *place* he was going ahead to prepare for us, *topos* (John 14:2). We must take responsibility and not give Satan space in our lives. Where we have done or do so, we need to repent and take that ground back from him. As we saw earlier, David gave space, through his many wives, to sexual weakness. This gave the devil a foothold. Judas gave the devil a foothold through his ongoing theft from the common purse. This seemingly small action ultimately led to his death. Weaknesses don't dictate our actions, just as we can't abdicate responsibility to Satan, but they can have a profound effect. We always have a choice, and it is never too late to repent and turn back to God.

Even after what Judas had done, there was a way back to God. The only thing that prevents our forgiveness and restoration with God is an unwillingness to acknowledge our sin and failure. As soon as he saw Jesus condemned, Judas realised what he had done. Distraught, he declared that he had sinned and shed innocent blood. He even returned the money to those who had paid him. It was an act of regret that could so easily have been an act of repentance and turning back to God. Yet for Judas his regret did not lead him to God; it led him to despair. Instead, overcome with guilt, he hung himself.

There is a parallel with people taking their own lives today. It's tragic that anyone can get to the point where they see no other option than to end things. We may be desperately in need of help to continue, but we never need to turn to something as final as suicide. There is never a moment when we can't turn to God, no matter how far away we feel or how far we have gone from him. Never, ever believe that you are beyond God's love or hope.[15]

In Luke's Gospel there is a wonderful story about a prodigal son (Luke 15). He abandoned his family, took his father's money and went in search of what he hoped would be a better life. But it all went horribly wrong. Drink, gambling and riches didn't make him happy and eventually his inheritance was squandered. But it was only when he was up to his knees in pig dung that he came to his senses and began the journey back to his father.

To his complete and utter shock, he found his father waiting, ready and expectant. In fact, his father didn't wait for him to get to the house. He came running out to meet him. He cut the son off mid-confession. He restored him to full belonging as his beloved child whom he had never given up on.

Recently I noticed something that I'd never seen before in the institution of the Last Supper. At the most holy moment, remembered in every communion service, Jesus interrupted and talked about Judas. 'This cup is the new covenant in my blood which is poured out for you. But the hand of him who is going to betray me is with mine on the table...' (Luke 22:20–21). Judas' betrayal came in the same sentence as Jesus spoke of the new covenant for the forgiveness of our sins. It was for all sins, even Judas', that Jesus died on the cross.

James and Judas/Thaddeus

We have two apostles left. There was James. This wasn't James the brother of John. This wasn't James the brother of Jesus. This was James the son of Alphaeus. Throughout history he would become known as James the Less. It appears that nothing is really known

---

15 If you are in any way struggling with the concept of carrying on with life, please talk to someone you trust or contact The Samaritans on 116123 or online via Samaritans.org

about him. He was just 'not this James or that James, but the other one'. And then there was Judas, who is called Judas in Luke, and Thaddeus in Matthew and Mark. In Luke and Acts he is called son of James. We know nothing about him and can't even really remember which was his preferred name. What a shame! You make it into the twelve and then don't do anything worthy enough of note. It's almost as if Jesus was just making up the numbers.

Although, with God, no one is simply making up the numbers. These guys got to be some of the closest people on earth to God himself. They spent three years with Jesus. They didn't just hear him teach; they knew him and he them. They did life, and later death, with him. That is significance enough.

8

The women in Jesus' life

Mary: Jesus' mother

At the start of this book, Liz said that I'd look at a woman. If you had to choose one woman in Scripture to focus on, there's no real choice. It has to be Mary, Jesus' mother. Speaking of who you'd choose, there was a brilliant head of Year 11 at a local high school where I used to help with the chaplaincy. This teacher did incredible year-group assemblies. He had clearly thought through what he wanted to communicate at each stage of the year, including a couple of times when he'd get personal and share his own testimony of faith.

Their final 'leavers' assembly' was always the most powerful. He would talk about working hard for their GCSEs and then he would put up a photo of a little boy and a little girl. He said that academic achievements, sporting accomplishments or other things were great, but they weren't as important as where the students stood in relation to these children. If a student was deemed a good enough person to babysit that boy and girl, then that was the greatest accolade they could ever have. He explained that the boy and girl were his children. If he would entrust his children to them, that said all you needed to know. It was a fantastic point. He'd seen these young people at their best and their worst, so allowing them to babysit would say a lot.

It says even more when I relate it to my own children. And when I put this in the context of Jesus, it takes things to a totally different dimension. God entrusted himself to a person, when he knew exactly what people were like. This teacher was looking at teenagers as potential babysitters. God looked at a teenage girl as the mother to his own Son. Not just to look after him, but to contribute to his eye colour and personality, to give birth to him and raise him. As the early Church set out to articulate our creeds and define the core doctrinal beliefs of the Church, knowing how to express the theology of the incarnation and Mary must have felt like an impossible task. For example, there was huge controversy around what to call her. A portion of the Church wanted to call her God-bearer – *theotokos* – but that seemed blasphemous to many. They simply couldn't understand that a woman could bear God. But it's only right that the incarnation should be too much for us to get our heads around.

The annunciation

Much is made of the distinctions between the angel Gabriel's appearance to Zechariah, who was John the Baptist's dad, and to Mary. Zechariah was a priest, a man of God. When the angel appeared to him, he was in the Temple offering incense, which was the closest anyone could get to God's presence on earth (Luke 1:8ff.). Surely, if you were going to encounter God, this was the time and place to expect it. In contrast, Mary was absorbed in the struggles of everyday life. The most significant thing she would have anticipated was her forthcoming marriage. Yet what happened when Gabriel appeared to them both is very similar. He told them not to be afraid, and he prophesied about not only a forthcoming pregnancy, but also the child's unique purpose and significance. Both of them struggled to believe what they were told. They would both later sing highly significant songs of praise and prophecy in response to the gift of a child.

There is, however, a subtle distinction in how they expressed their disbelief and the discourse that followed. Zechariah replied to Gabriel, 'How can I be sure of this? I am an old man and my wife is well on in years' (Luke 1:18). While Mary said, 'How will this be …

since I am a virgin?' (Luke 1:34). Both gave a physical reason why it couldn't happen. But Zechariah focused on himself (How will I?) and Mary focused on the event (How will this be?).

In terms of proof, Zechariah immediately lost the ability to speak. I love the fact that, at this point, the privileged priest is silenced while we get to hear the most remarkable reply of a normal teenage girl. She responded, 'I am the Lord's servant … May your word to me be fulfilled' (Luke 1:38). Her response was mirrored in Jesus' response as he prepared for the crucifixion and said, 'Not my will, but yours be done' (Luke 22:42).

I'd like to think that I'm alert to God when I'm in a spiritual place, such as preparing a sermon or praying. I'm especially alert when praying for someone else. I'm constantly on call when on a train, ready for a prompting from God that will change someone's life. Yet, I'm not so sure that my ears are open to God when loading the dishwasher, doing the weekly shop or sitting on the sofa at home. This makes me question how available I am to God in the everyday of life.

I meet many priests who, rather than exuding faith, have had their faith eroded over the years. I worry that we are more likely to say what won't work or happen than to declare what God can do. Mary went on to sing her most famous song, which speaks of God's faithfulness and promise in ways that hadn't been seen by Israel in her lifetime. All she would ever have seen in practice was the rich getting richer and the poor being more afflicted and increasingly worse off.

Can we, like Mary, declare such hope and truth even when it isn't what we have seen with our own eyes? Does our faith – being sure of what we hope for and certain of what we do not see – hold up in spite of what we see on the news and in our communities?

Jesus was born

The Christmas story is so familiar to us. Although it's probably best known through the lens of nativities full of children in dressing gowns and tea towels clutching baby dolls, for Mary, Jesus' birth must have been both a terrifying and a phenomenal time. The stress of giving birth, followed immediately by the appearance of shepherds. As soon as the shepherds left, we are told that 'Mary treasured up all these things and pondered them in her heart' (Luke 2:19).

We only hear about two other incidents in Jesus' childhood. The first is when they took him to the Temple as a baby, and Anna and Simeon prophesied over the boy Jesus. Simeon said that a sword would pierce Mary's soul (verse 35). The other is the memorable time when they lost Jesus as a boy at the Temple. On their return, again it says that Mary 'treasured all these things in her heart' (verse 51). The Greek words used for 'treasuring in her heart' speak of guarding and holding near. The word for pondering literally means 'throw with or about'. It's about wrestling or disputing. Mary reflected deeply on all that was happening as Jesus grew up. She held it deep in her heart as something precious, but it wasn't all a joyful treasure. There was also pain and confusion. In an even more profound way than we experience as Christians, her experience was that being with Jesus is amazing, but not always straightforward or easy.

When I was a teenager, almost the first verse you learned as a new Christian, which summed up faith, was John 3:16. Over the last decade, I think John 10:10 has become more likely to be used. Our understanding of Christian faith has moved from being about our need for Jesus to save us to being about Jesus giving us a fuller life. But there is a huge danger that the idea of life to the full is misunderstood. Life to the full isn't just about God making life feel better.

A friend of mine has spent the last two years trying to support his wife through the most profound trauma. He said that they have been the toughest years of his life and yet they have felt the most full. Fullness of life is not just about the highs, but it's the full bandwidth of being truly alive. Giving life to Jesus, and spending her life with him, meant that Mary experienced more pain and distress than she would ever otherwise have known. But she didn't avoid that pain; she pondered it. She wrestled with it. We sell people a lie if we simply say that Christianity will make them happy and protect them from pain.

Letting go of her son

All parenting is about letting go of our children as they grow up and become independent. Some would say that you know you've made it as a parent when you're lying awake worrying about them while they swan around without a second thought to what you're doing.

For Mary, a key moment of letting go came at a family wedding. Jesus was there with her, but he already had disciples by this time, and they were there too. It's as if he was between the two worlds. The wine ran out, and Mary asked Jesus to intervene to prevent the shame that would hound this young couple for the rest of their lives. To be fair, she didn't exactly ask, but she pointed the problem out to Jesus (mum-speak for 'You need to do something'). Jesus responded, 'Woman, why do you involve me? … My hour has not yet come' (John 2:4).

The term 'woman' wasn't as harsh as it might sound to us today. It could be used affectionately. But this incident does speak of a shift in their relationship. At twelve, when he was left behind in the Temple, he was in his Father's house, but he still followed her when she came back for him. But at that wedding, it was no longer her place to direct his life. Mary would stay close to Jesus throughout his ministry (Matthew 12:46), but she would end up following him, rather than him following her.

Of even greater note in this story is the reference to his 'hour'. In John's Gospel, 'hour' always refers to the cross. At the wedding, Jesus met the immediate physical needs of the people when no one else could. Then, when his hour came, he would pour out his blood for all people, and meet a need no one else could. This first miracle is said to be 'the first of the signs through which he revealed his glory' (John 2:11). 'Glory' is the other word John uses to refer to the cross. All of Jesus' life was inextricably linked to the cross, as was Mary's. Mary couldn't get away from what he'd come to do. It was there that her soul would be pierced. The cost to her was greater than anyone else's, with the exception of God the Father himself. She raised her son to die.

Mary's only other appearance in John's Gospel is at the cross. Here again, Jesus addressed her as 'woman'. At his moment of greatest need, when he was contending with the needs of the world, he looked to Mary's needs. Even though she had other children, he asked his closest disciple, John, to take her as his mother. There was something so intimate about that action from the cross, as it expressed something of the intimate love and care Jesus has for us all.

Pentecost

Let's conclude by looking at the last place Mary appears, in Acts. In Acts 1:14, we read that the apostles 'joined together constantly in prayer, along with the women and Mary the mother of Jesus, and with his brothers'. According to Luke, there were about 120 believers there, including Mary (Acts 1:15).

Then in Acts 2 Pentecost comes. I don't know how you picture Pentecost. In my imagination, there was a jump. One minute they were locked away in the upper room, with the sound of the wind and tongues of fire settling on them. Then, without even realising what was going on, they were out in the street, with everyone commenting on the tongues they were speaking in rather than the tongues of fire on their heads. If I'm honest, in that leap between the two scenes I totally lose any concept of 108 people. That might be because whereas Acts 2 begins, 'When the day of Pentecost came, they were all together in one place,' in verse 14 it says that Peter stood up with the eleven to preach. I'm embarrassed to say I've only just realised that in my mind Pentecost is about the twelve, but the exact opposite is true.

One of the earliest surviving pieces of art depicting Pentecost is in the sixth-century Rabbula Gospels. It has Mary at the centre, with six apostles on either side. She was there. Acts tells us so. In fact, the art doesn't even get it right, because it leaves out the 107 nameless people who also received the gift of the Holy Spirit and of tongues.

Pentecost was for all believers. God doesn't pick and choose the best ones, the most sorted ones, to call, empower and use. He calls each one of us. It's his gift of himself within us. That is what enables us to follow him, let alone lead as he would have us lead. It is also by that Spirit that God effects change in our lives. He binds our broken hearts and lives. He slowly makes us more like Jesus. It's how he can take a teenage girl and, through her, literally change history. Mary's story began and ended with the Holy Spirit coming upon her. He does that with us too.

Conclusion

What about us?

Introduction

For Peter, it didn't matter how far he walked on water. It was the fact that he alone could say he walked on water. It doesn't matter if we know a lot, or indeed anything, about the minor apostles. The fact is that they were Jesus' disciples. The same is true with us. God is less worried about what you do with him than that you have a relationship with him. He doesn't call us to be famous or change the whole world. He calls us to follow him where we are, as the people we are. He wants us to recognise that Jesus is the solution to our failure. He died on the cross for all that we have done wrong and ever will do wrong.

The cross seemed like the greatest failure in history. On the cross God himself was put to death for other people's wrongdoing. But really, the cross was the solution to all failure in history. Jesus rose again, and in his death and resurrection conquered sin and death. Jesus died and rose again so that we might have a relationship with God. A relationship that he will never give up on and that lasts for eternity. This relationship begins when we acknowledge that we are, in some way, failures who need forgiveness and restoration, and therefore choose to give our lives back to him. If you don't think you have that relationship, or once had it but have given up on it, I wholeheartedly commend that you do something about that now as you finish this book.[1]

---

1 Pray – talk to God. Be honest and real with him. Pick up a Bible and get reading – maybe start with a gospel (Matthew, Mark, Luke or John). You might also want to talk to a trusted Christian friend or church leader. You could try a local church. If you go to one that isn't welcoming or keen to help, don't give up, try another!

The Bible is full of examples of flawed faithfulness. Its characters are both heroes and failures. God doesn't measure success or significance, or even failure, as the world does. You can read this for yourself in this description, taken from a sermon preached a hundred years ago, of Jesus, God himself, whom we follow:

Here is a man who was born in an obscure village, the child of a peasant woman. He grew up in another village. He worked in a carpenter shop until he was thirty. Then for three years he was an itinerant preacher. He never owned a home. He never wrote a book. He never held office. He never had a family. He never went to college. He never put his foot inside a big city. He never travelled two hundred miles from the place he was born. He never did one of the things that usually accompany greatness. He had no credentials but himself...

While still a young man, the tide of popular opinion turned against him. His friends ran away. One of them denied him. He was turned over to his enemies. He went through the mockery of a trial. He was nailed upon a cross between two thieves. While he was dying, his executioners gambled for the only piece of property he had on earth – his coat. When he was dead, he was laid in a borrowed grave through the pity of a friend.

Nineteen long centuries have come and gone, and today he is a centrepiece of the human race and leader of the column of progress. I am far within the mark when I say that all the armies that ever marched, all the navies that were ever built, all the parliaments that ever sat and all the kings that ever reigned, put together, have not affected the life of man upon this earth as powerfully as has that one solitary life.[2]

---

2 Adapted from a sermon, 'Arise Sir Knight!', by Dr James Allan Francis in *The Real Jesus and Other Sermons* (Philadelphia: Judson Press, 1926), pp. 123–24.

There are no qualifications needed to be a friend of God. We never need to prove ourselves to him. We don't need to be more like anyone else. We need to be ourselves and then give our lives to the God who loves us and accepts us. The God who can heal all our failures, and the failures of others that have hurt and broken us. I would urge you not to let anything hold you back or away from God. Come as you are and be changed for ever. Then you can spend a lifetime discovering the fullness of life that God gives you. You too can be one of God's normal, imperfect heroes.

Acknowledgements

This book focuses predominantly on men, but my greatest debt of gratitude goes to women. So let's get the men out of the way and then focus on those women.

I am very grateful to two men in particular. I struggle to say 'men' rather than 'boys', but they are indeed men, and pretty impressive men at that. Josh and Toby, thank you for all your hard work to keep me humble, but most of all for being more than we could have ever hoped or prayed for.

I'm also profoundly grateful to Matt Summerfield, my mentor, for his unceasing support, wisdom and encouragement. Then there is the leader who has probably had the most impact on Liz and me from before we even started going out – David MacInnes and his wife Clare. Thank you for the wonderful example you have always been and all your support over the years.

I also need to acknowledge and give thanks for everyone involved with Unlimited over the years. You shaped us as leaders probably more than we shaped you!

And now to the three women:

First and foremost – Liz. This is just the tip of the iceberg of your love, support, encouragement and general brilliance. This book wouldn't exist without you. You literally made it happen. You believed in the concept and then developed my splurge of thoughts into a coherent book. Your academic prowess and ever-growing theological wisdom were reasonably useful too! You are the most amazing person, woman, wife, mother and friend, and I get to be your husband. Thank you!

Second – Lauren. I have to confess I was somewhat dubious about someone editing the book. It was bad enough having Liz rework it, let alone someone I didn't know. But you have been amazing. Annoyingly, I've read so many bits of the book and thought how well I expressed things, only to realise that it's your fantastic turn of phrase, not mine! Thank you for your way with words and being a normal, imperfect glass-slipper-wearing hero. Be encouraged!

Third – my mother! Everyone thanks their mum and this is no exception. My mum constantly worries about whether she could have done better as a parent, and takes any struggles I have ever had upon herself. Hopefully this book will encourage you that while we all have weaknesses and failings, God uses us in wonderful ways in spite of them. And I think you've done a pretty good job as a parent!

And now over to Liz...

My first acknowledgement, of course, has to go to my husband, James. It is inevitable when you are married to a vicar that the majority of your teaching comes from your spouse. Over thirty years I have sat through innumerable sermons, countless small-group talks and many seminars, all by you. Yet it never gets old. You continually find new insights in the Bible that excite you, and new ways to communicate. My love of Scripture, in particular the Old Testament, is in no small part due to you and your teaching. It was a privilege when you begrudgingly let me loose on your forgotten manuscript. The trust you placed in me was immense and it has been great to work with you on this project.

Lauren, you have worked a miracle. You have taken James's words and helped him sound even more like himself. You have reduced this manuscript by 20,000 words, and for James to not merely not mind but actually approve, you have been more than reasonably useful! Thank you for such a joyful experience.

Both of us owe an immeasurable debt to our two sons. Josh and Toby, you help us at every level to keep it real. We are never allowed to get away with sloppy or lazy theology. You equally never let us get away with moments when our behaviour is not in line with our teaching. Even when you were little you regularly humbled me and sent me to my knees in prayer. My faith is deepened by you almost daily. (I say 'almost', because now you no longer live at home you don't always remember to get in touch…) You question us at every level. Boys, your love of Scripture is an inspiration to me, and I pray that you will continue to ask the hard questions of it and of us. It is also a source of delight to me that I am now not the only girl in our discussions, as Beccah joins you in your love of Scripture and questioning.

I am also immensely grateful to all the people in my life who have supported and encouraged me over the years. I can't name everyone, but a few do merit a special mention. First, Jo, my closest friend, who has done life in all its fullness with me, and together we have weathered the toughest of times and enjoyed the craziest of celebrations. Second, my spiritual director Sharon, who always quietly listens as I verbally place everything out on the carpet and wisely helps me see where God is in everything. Third, my fellow pray-ers Jo and Sarah – we can be scatty with our meetings, but your godly wisdom, faith and willingness to trust God as you work out your calling is inspirational. And it would not be right not to mention the wonderful people at Trinity College, the DLs (Andy C., Andy S., Emma, Gill, Nick, Sarah, Sue, Catherine, David, Rob, Joel, Nicola, Simon, Tracey) and GLs (you know who you are), with whom it has been the greatest honour to be shaped as we learn about godly leadership – thank you for all the wisdom, laughter and encouragement.

And finally, my love of the Old Testament, started by my husband's preaching, has been deepened and enriched immeasurably by my supervisor David Firth. I never intended to do a PhD in theology. I would never have considered for a second that I was up to the task – or that I was capable of learning Hebrew. I am forever thankful that David did not share my opinion and endlessly encourages me to keep on going, to keep on asking questions. He continually brings me back to task and never lets me get overwhelmed by the size of the mountain ahead, fixing my gaze instead on God alone. And my thanks must also go to James Harding, who bravely took on an unknown curate and trusted me with both ordinands and lectures. It is the greatest of joys to be both teaching the Old Testament and helping to shape godly leaders for this country.

But more than any of these people, my thanks go to God. Who calls me by name and who loves me as a daughter, and who promises to always be with me wherever I am called.